ANALYZING THE ISSUES

CRITICAL PERSPECTIVES ON
FREE TRADE AND
GLOBALIZATION

Edited by Bridey Heing

Enslow Publishing

101 W. 23rd Street
Suite 240
New York, NY 10011
USA

enslow.com

Published in 2018 by Enslow Publishing, LLC
101 W. 23rd Street, Suite 240, New York, NY 10011

Library of Congress Cataloging-in-Publication Data

Names: Heing, Bridey, editor.
Title: Critical perspectives on free trade and globalization / edited by
  Bridey Heing.
Description: New York : Enslow Publishing, [2018] | Series: Analyzing the
  issues | Audience: Grades 7-12. | Includes bibliographical references and
  index.
Identifiers: LCCN 2017011510 | ISBN 9780766091689 (library bound)
  | ISBN 9780766095595 (paperback)
Subjects: LCSH: Free trade—Juvenile literature. | International economic
  relations—Juvenile literature.
Classification: LCC HF1713 .C696 2017 | DDC 382/.71—dc23
LC record available at https://lccn.loc.gov/2017011510

Printed in China

Photo Credits: Cover mf-guddyx/E+/Getty Images; cover and interior
pages graphic elements Thaiview/Shutterstock.com (cover top, pp. 1, 4–5),
gbreezy/Shutterstock.com (magnifying glass), Ghornstern/Shutterstock.com
(additional interior pages).

CONTENTS

INTRODUCTION

International trade is the driving force of the global economy, bringing new products to every corner of the world and connecting people in exciting new ways. Trade deals between countries are one of the most effective ways to build relationships, and trade relations help maintain peace between nations. But international trade is also a significant source of controversy, with a great deal of debate about how countries can best negotiate trade deals that benefit both workers and consumers.

Free trade has been a particularly heavily debated issue in recent decades. Free trade is a type of agreement that removes tariffs (or a tax paid on imports and exports) and other financial restrictions associated with trading between countries. According to economists, this kind of trade helps promote business between countries by providing economic incentives to companies that want to import or export goods.

The United States has free trade agreements with about twenty countries, ranging from Bahrain to Chile. Two large free trade agreements cover multiple countries—Mexico and Canada are part of the North American Free Trade Agreement (NAFTA), while Costa Rica, the Dominican Republic, El Salvador, Guatemala, Honduras, and Nicaragua are all signatories on the Dominican Republic-

Central America-United States Free Trade Agreement (DR-CAFTA). Trade with these countries accounts for around 47 percent of all US exports, totaling around $710 billion in 2015 according to the International Trade Administration.[1]

Advocates, including many economists, believe that by removing barriers to trade the economy is strengthened. Competition is also increased by free trade, which many believe will drive companies to be more innovative and keep costs low for consumers. But opponents of free trade worry that these deals undercut US workers and businesses, as well as developing countries, by making it difficult for them to compete against major economic players. Many, including politicians on both the left and right, have expressed concern that cheap foreign imports drive costs too low for local manufacturers to compete, and the lack of tariffs on goods incentivizes companies to move to countries with low production costs.

Globalization goes hand-in-hand with free trade. Globalization is the process by which countries and populations interact and share goods, ideas, and culture. By doing so, our world becomes more connected and the economies of all countries become more closely woven together. Globalization is an important part of free trade; as companies are able to do business with other countries more easily, goods and services should bring countries closer together. But many are concerned that globalization can obscure the native cultures of smaller countries, and companies can take advantage of workers in countries with poor regulations while not bringing significant economic gains to those countries.

Politics also plays an important role in this debate, which involves countries from around the world. From China to India to Europe, relations between the United States and allies are largely shaped by trade relations; in the case of China, it was trade that opened the door to normalized relations in the 1970s. While trade can make the world safer, it is also a complicated reflection of where countries stand on issues, leading to debates on whether or not we should trade with countries that do not reflect our values.

Free trade and globalization might be in the news a lot these days, but neither of these concepts are new. Trade and the exchanging of culture that comes with it has been driving human civilization and progress since ancient times. Free trade, or trade with fewer tariffs and restrictions, has been part of international trade for centuries, but was introduced in the United States in 1934 when President Franklin D. Roosevelt began negotiating trade deals that brought down costs so that United States manufacturers could more easily do business overseas. Because of free trade agreements, tariffs fell from 60 percent in 1930 to 2.7 percent in 2013.[2]

Trade policy is discussed and debated at all levels of society, from the halls of government where trade deals are made to conversations between people across the country who are impacted directly and indirectly by changes in trade agreements. In this collection, we'll hear from academics, economists, presidents, and concerned citizens, all of whom have different opinions and views on how free trade and globalization are shaping our world and country.

CHAPTER 1

WHAT ACADEMICS, EXPERTS, AND RESEARCHERS SAY

F ree trade and its impact on the economy has been researched widely by universities, economists, governments, and other organizations interested in developing the most successful trade policy possible. But that does not mean that all research reaches the same conclusions; in fact, while there is a great deal of agreement between economists about the benefits of free trade, those who approach the subject from different stances (such as environmental or cultural) have raised concerns about the potential damage free trade can do. In this chapter, we will examine the history of free trade around the world, recent changes in public opinion about free trade, and how globalization and free trade have shaped our world.

EXCERPT FROM "KICKING AWAY THE LADDER: THE 'REAL' HISTORY OF FREE TRADE," BY HA-JOON CHANG, FROM *FOREIGN POLICY IN FOCUS*, DECEMBER 30, 2013

Central to the neoliberal discourse on globalization is the conviction that free trade, more than free movements of capital or labor, is the key to global prosperity. Even many of those who are not enthusiastic about all aspects of globalization—ranging from the free-trade economist, Jagdish Bhagwati, advocating capital control to some non-governmental organizations (NGOs) accusing the developed countries for not opening up their agricultural markets—seem to agree that free trade is the most benign, or at least a less problematic, element in the progress of globalization.

Part of the conviction in free trade that the proponents of globalization possess comes from the belief that economic theory has irrefutably established the superiority of free trade, even though there are some formal models which show free trade may not be the best. However, even the builders of those models, such as Paul Krugman, argue that free trade is still the best policy because interventionist trade policies are almost certain to be politically abused. Even more powerful for the proponents of free trade, is their belief that history is on their side. After all, the defenders of free trade ask, isn't free trade how all the world's developed countries have become rich? What are some developing countries thinking, they wonder, when they refuse to adopt such a tried and tested recipe for economic development?

A closer look at the history of capitalism, however, reveals a very different story (Chang, 2002). As we shall establish in some detail in this paper, when they were developing countries themselves, virtually all of today's developed countries did not practice free trade (and *laissez-faire* industrial policy as its domestic counterpart). Rather, they promoted their national industries through tariffs, subsidies, and other measures. Particularly notable is the fact that the gap between "real" and "imagined" histories of trade policy is the greatest in relation to Britain and the United States, which are conventionally believed to have reached the top of the world's economic hierarchy by adopting free trade when other countries were stuck with outdated mercantilist policies. These two countries were, in fact, often the pioneers and frequently the most ardent users of *interventionist* trade and industrial policy measures in their early stages of development.

Debunking the myth of free trade from the historical perspective demonstrates that there is an urgent need for thoroughly re-thinking some key conventional wisdom in the debate on trade policy, and more broadly on globalization.

THE "OFFICIAL HISTORY OF CAPITALISM" AND ITS LIMITATIONS

The "official history of capitalism," which informs today's debate on trade policy, economic development, and globalization, goes like the following.

From the eighteenth century, Britain proved the superiority of free-market and free-trade policies by beating interventionist France, its main competitor at the time, and establishing itself as the supreme world economic power. Especially once it had abandoned its deplorable agricultural protection (the Corn Law) and other remnants of old mercantilist protectionist measures in 1846, it was able to play the role of the architect and dominant influence of a new "liberal" world economic order. This liberal world order, perfected around 1870, was based on *laissez-faire* industrial policies at home; low barriers to the international flows of goods, capital, and labor; and macroeconomic stability, both nationally and internationally, guaranteed by the Gold Standard and the principle of balanced budgets. A period of unprecedented prosperity followed.

Unfortunately, according to this story, things started to go wrong with the First World War. In response to the ensuing instability of the world economic and political system, countries started to erect trade barriers again. In 1930, the United States also abandoned free trade and raised tariffs with the infamous Smoot-Hawley tariff, which Jagdish Bhagwati called "the most visible and dramatic act of anti-trade folly" (Bhagwati, 1985, p. 22, footnote 10). The world free trade system finally ended in 1932, when Britain, hitherto the champion of free trade, succumbed to the temptation and re-introduced tariffs. The resulting contraction and instability in the world economy, and then finally the Second World War, destroyed the last remnants of the first liberal world order.

After the Second World War, so the story goes, some significant progress was made in trade liberalization through the early General Agreement on Trade and Tariffs (GATT) talks. However, unfortunately, *dirigiste* approaches to economic management dominated the policy-making scene until the 1970s in the developed world, and until the early 1980s in the developing world (and the Communist world until its collapse in 1989).

Fortunately, it is said, interventionist policies have been largely abandoned across the world since the 1980s with the rise of neoliberalism, which emphasized the virtues of small government, *laissez-faire* policies, and international openness. Especially in the developing world, by the late 1970s economic growth had begun to falter in most countries outside East and Southeast Asia, which were already pursuing "good" policies (of free market and free trade). This growth failure, which often manifested itself in economic crises of the early 1980s, exposed the limitations of old-style interventionism and protectionism. As a result, most developing countries have come to embrace "policy reform" in a neoliberal direction.

When combined with the establishment of new global governance institutions, represented by the World Trade Organization (WTO), these policy changes at the national level have created a new global economic system, comparable in its potential prosperity only to the earlier "golden age" of liberalism (1870–1914). Renato Ruggiero, the first director-general of the WTO, thus argues that, thanks to this new world order, we now have "the potential for eradicating global poverty in the early part of the next [twenty-first] century–a utopian notion even a few decades ago, but a real possibility today" (1998, p. 131).

As we shall see later, this story paints a fundamentally misleading picture, but no less a powerful one for it. And it should be accepted that there are some senses in which the late nineteenth century can indeed be described as a *laissez-faire* era.

To begin with, there was a period in the late-nine-teenth century, albeit a brief one, when liberal trade regimes prevailed in large parts of the world economy. Between 1860 and 1880, many European countries reduced tariff protection substantially [...] At the same time, most of the rest of the world was forced to practice free trade through colonialism and through unequal treaties in the cases of a few nomi-nally "independent" countries (such as the Latin American countries, China, Thailand [then Siam], Iran [then Persia], and Turkey [then the Ottoman Empire], and even Japan until 1911). Of course, the obvious exception to this was the United States, which maintained very high tariff barriers even during this period [...] However, given that the United States was still a relatively small part of the world economy, it may not be totally unreasonable to say that this is as close to free trade as the world has ever come.

More importantly, the scope of state intervention before the First World War was quite limited by modern standards. States had limited budgetary policy capa-bility because there was no income tax in most countries and the balanced budget doctrine dominated. They also had limited monetary policy capability because many of them did not have a central bank, and the Gold Standard restricted their policy freedom. They also had limited command over investment resources, as they owned or regulated few financial institutions and industrial enter-prises. One somewhat paradoxical consequence of all these limitations was that tariff protection was far more important as a policy tool in the nineteenth century than it is in our time.

Despite these limitations, as we shall soon see, virtu-ally all of today's developed countries—or now-developed countries (henceforth NDCs)–actively used interventionist trade and industrial policies aimed at promoting, not simply "protecting," it should be emphasized, infant industries during their catch-up periods.

Britain was the first country to introduce a permanent income tax, which happened in 1842. Denmark introduced income tax in 1903. In the United States, the income tax law of 1894 was overturned as "unconstitutional" by the Supreme Court. The Sixteenth Amendment, allowing federal income tax, was adopted only in 1913. In Belgium, income tax was introduced only in 1919. In Portugal, income tax was first introduced in 1922, but was abolished in 1928, and re-instated only in 1933. In Sweden, despite its later fame for the willingness to impose high rates of income tax, income tax was first introduced only in 1932. See Chang (2002, p. 101) for further details.

The Swedish Riksbank was nominally the first official central bank in the world (established in 1688), but until the mid-nineteenth century, it could not function as a proper central bank because it did not have monopoly over note issue, which it acquired only in 1904. The first "real" central bank was the Bank of England, which was established in 1694, but became a full central bank in 1844. By the end of the nineteenth century, the central banks of France (1848), Belgium (1851), Spain (1874), and Portugal (1891) gained note issue monopoly, but it was only in the twentieth century that the central banks of Germany (1905), Switzerland (1907), and Italy (1926) gained it. The Swiss National Bank was formed only in 1907 by merging the four note-issue banks. The U.S. Federal Reserve System came into being only in 1913. Until 1915, however, only 30% of the banks (with 50% of all banking assets) were in the system, and even as late as 1929, 65% of the banks were still outside the system, although by this time they accounted for only 20% of total banking assets. See Chang (2002, pp. 94–97) for further details.

Moreover, when they reached the frontier, the NDCs used a range of policies in order to help themselves "pull away" from their existing and potential competitors. They used measures to control transfer of technology to its potential competitors (e.g., controls on skilled worker migration or machinery export) and made the less developed countries open up their markets by unequal treaties and colonization. However, the catch-up economies that were not formal or informal colonies did not simply sit down and accept these restrictive measures. They mobilized all kinds of different "legal" and "illegal" means to overcome the obstacles created by these restrictions, such as industrial espionage, poaching of workers, and smuggling of contraband machinery. See Chang (2002, pp. 51–9) for further details.

HISTORY OF TRADE AND INDUSTRIAL POLICIES IN TODAY'S DEVELOPED COUNTRIES

BRITAIN

As the intellectual fountain of the modern *laissez-faire* doctrines and as the only country that can claim to have practiced a total free trade at least at one point, Britain is widely regarded as having developed without significant state intervention. However, this cannot be further from the truth.

Britain entered its post-feudal age (thirteenth to fourteenth centuries) as a relatively backward economy. It relied on exports of raw wool and, to a lesser extent, of low-value-added wool cloth to the then more advanced Low Countries (Ramsay, 1982, p. 59; Davies, 1999, p. 348). Edward III (1312–1377) is believed to have been the first king who deliberately tried to develop local wool cloth manufacturing. He only wore English cloth to set an example, brought in the Flemish weavers, centralized trade in raw wool, and banned the import of woolen cloth (Davies, 1999, p. 349; Davis, 1966, p. 281).

Further impetus came from the Tudor monarchs. The famous eighteenth-century merchant, politician, and the author of the novel, *Robinson Crusoe*, Daniel Defoe, describes this policy in his now-almost-forgotten book, *A Plan of the English Commerce* (1728). In this book, he describes in some detail how the Tudor monarchs, especially Henry VII (1485–1509), transformed England from a raw-wool exporter into the most formidable woolen-manufacturing nation in the world (pp. 81–101). According to Defoe, from 1489, Henry VII implemented schemes to promote woolen manufacturing, which included sending royal missions to identify locations suited to wool manufacturing; poaching skilled workers from the Low Countries; increasing duties on the export of raw wool; and even temporarily banning the export of raw wool (Ramsay, 1982, provides further details).

For obvious reasons, it is difficult to establish the exact importance of the above-mentioned infant industry promotion policies. However, without them, it would have been very difficult for Britain to make this initial success in industrialization, without which its Industrial Revolution may have been next to impossible.

The most important event in Britain's industrial development, however, was the 1721 policy reform introduced by Robert Walpole, the first British prime minister, during the reign of George I (1660–1727). Prior to this, the British government's policies were, in general, aimed at capturing trade and generating government revenue. Even the promotion of woolen manufacturing was partly motivated by revenue considerations. In contrast, the policies introduced after 1721 were deliberately aimed at promoting manufacturing industries. Introducing the new law, Walpole stated, through the king's address to the Parliament: "it is evident that nothing so much contributes to promote the public well-being as the exportation of manufactured goods and the importation of foreign raw material" (as cited in List, 1885, p. 40).

The 1721 legislation, and the supplementary policy changes subsequently made, included the following measures (for details, see Brisco, 1907, pp. 131–33, p. 148–55, pp. 169–71; McCusker, 1996, p. 358; Davis, 1966, pp. 313–4). First of all, import duties on raw materials used for manufactures were lowered, or even altogether dropped. Second, duty drawbacks on imported raw materials for exported manufactures were increased. Third, export duties on most manufactures were abolished. Fourth, duties on imported foreign manufactured goods were raised. Fifth, export subsidies (then called "bounties") were extended to new export items like silk products and gunpowder, while the existing export subsidies to sailcloth and refined sugar were increased. Sixth, regulation was introduced to control the quality of manufactured products, especially textile products, so that unscrupulous manufacturers would not damage the reputation of British products in foreign markets. What is very interesting is that these policies, as well as the principles behind them, were uncannily similar to those used by countries like Japan, Korea, and Taiwan during the post-war period (see below).

Despite its widening technological lead over other countries, Britain continued its policies of industrial promotion until the mid-nineteenth century [...] Britain had very high tariffs on manufacturing products even as late as the 1820s, some two generations after the start of its Industrial Revolution.

By the end of the Napoleonic War in 1815, however, there were increasing pressures for free trade in Britain from the increasingly confident manufacturers. Although there was a round of tariff reduction in 1833, the big change came in 1846, when the Corn Law was repealed and tariffs on many manufacturing goods abolished (Bairoch, 1993, pp. 20–21).

The repeal of the Corn Law is now commonly regarded as the ultimate victory of the classical liberal economic doctrine over wrong-headed mercantilism. Although we should not underestimate the role of economic theory in this policy shift, it is probably better understood as an act of "free trade imperialism" (the term is due to Gallagher & Robinson, 1953) intended to "halt the move to industrialization on the Continent by enlarging the market for agricultural produce and primary materials" (Kindleberger, 1978, p. 196). Indeed, many leaders of the campaign to repeal the Corn Law, such as the politician Richard Cobden and John Bowring of the Board of Trade, saw their campaign precisely in such terms (Kindleberger, 1975, and Reinert, 1998). Cobden's view on this is clearly revealed in the following passage: "The factory system would, in all probability, not have taken place in America and Germany. It most certainly could not have flourished, as it has done, both in these states, and in France, Belgium, and Switzer-land, through the fostering bounties which the high-priced food of the British artisan has offered to the cheaper fed manufacturer of those countries" (*The Political Writings of Richard Cobden*, 1868, William Ridgeway, London, vol. 1, p. 150; as cited in Reinert, 1998, p. 292).

Symbolic as the repeal of the Corn Law may have been, it was only after 1860 that most tariffs were abolished. However, the era of free trade did not last very long. It ended when Britain finally acknowledged that it had lost its manu-facturing eminence and re-introduced tariffs on a large scale in 1932 (Bairoch, 1993, pp. 27–8).

Thus seen, contrary to the popular belief, Britain 's technological lead that enabled this shift to a free trade regime had been achieved "behind high and long-lasting tariff barriers" (Bairoch, 1993, p. 46). And it is for this reason that Friedrich List, the nineteenth-century German econo-mist who is mistakenly [...] known as the father of modern "infant industry" theory, wrote the following passages.

"It is a very common clever device that when anyone has attained the summit of greatness, he *kicks away the ladder* by which he has climbed up, in order to deprive others of the means of climbing up after him. In this lies the secret of the cosmopolitical doctrine of Adam Smith, and of the cosmopolitical tendencies of his great contemporary William Pitt, and of all his successors in the British Government administrations.

Any nation which by means of protective duties and restrictions on navigation has raised her manufacturing power and her navigation to such a degree of develop-ment that no other nation can sustain free competition with her, can do nothing wiser than to throw away these ladders of her greatness, to preach to other nations the benefits of free trade, and to declare in penitent tones that she has hitherto wandered in the paths of error, and has now for the first time succeeded in discovering the truth [italics added]" (List, 1885, pp. 295–6).

UNITED STATES OF AMERICA

As we have just seen, Britain was the first country to successfully use a large-scale infant industry promotion strategy. However, its most ardent user was probably the U.S.; the eminent economic historian Paul Bairoch once called it "the mother country and bastion of modern protectionism" (Bairoch, 1993, p. 30). This fact is, interestingly, rarely acknowledged in the modern literature, especially coming out of the United States. However, the importance of infant industry protection in U.S. development cannot be over-emphasized.

From the early days of colonization, industrial protection was a controversial policy issue. To begin with, Britain did not want to industrialize the American colonies, and duly implemented policies to that effect (e.g., banning of high-value-added manufacturing activities). Around the time of independence, the southern agrarian interests opposed any protection, and the northern manufacturing interests wanted it, represented by, among others, Alexander Hamilton, the first Secretary of the Treasury of the United States (1789–1795).

In fact, it was Alexander Hamilton in his *Reports of the Secretary of the Treasury on the Subject of Manufactures* (1791) who first systematically set out the infant industry argument, and not the German economist Friedrich List, as it is often thought (Corden, 1974, ch. 8; Reinert, 1996). Indeed, List started out as a free trade advocate and only converted to the infant industry argument following his exile in the U.S (1825–1830) (Henderson, 1983, Reinert, 1998). Many U.S. intellectuals and politicians during the country's catch-up period clearly understood that the free trade theory advocated by the British classical economists was unsuited to their country. Indeed, it was against the advice of great economists like Adam Smith and Jean Baptiste Say that the Americans were protecting their industries.

In his *Reports*, Hamilton argued that the competition from abroad and the "forces of habit" would mean that new industries that could soon become internationally competitive ("infant industries") would not be started in the United States, unless the initial losses were guaranteed by government aid (Dorfman & Tugwell, 1960, pp. 31–32; Conkin, 1980, pp. 176–77). According to him, this aid could take the form of import duties or, in rare cases, prohibition of imports (Dorfman & Tugwell, 1960, p. 32). He also believed that duties on raw materials should be generally low (p. 32). We can see close resemblance between this view and the view espoused by Walpole [...] a point that was not lost on the contemporary Americans, especially Hamilton's political opponents (Elkins & McKitrick, 1993, p. 19).

Initially, the United States did not have a federal-level tariff system, but when the Congress acquired the power to tax, it passed a liberal tariff act (1789), imposing a 5% flat rate tariff on all imports, with some exceptions (Garraty & Carnes, 2000, pp. 139–40, p. 153; Bairoch, 1993, p. 33). And despite Hamilton's *Reports*, between 1792 and the war with Britain in 1812, the average tariff level remained around 12.5%, although during the war all tariffs were doubled in order to meet the increased government expenses due to the war (p. 210).

A significant shift in policy occurred in 1816, when a new law was introduced to keep the tariff level close to the wartime level—especially protected were cotton, woolen, and iron goods (Garraty & Carnes, 2000, p. 210; Cochran & Miller, 1942, pp. 15–16). Between 1816 and the end of the Second World War, the U.S. had one of the highest average tariff rates on manufacturing imports in the world [...] Given that the country enjoyed an exceptionally high degree of "natural" protection due to high transportation costs at least until the 1870s, we can say that the U.S. industries were literally the most protected in the world until 1945.

Even the Smoot-Hawley Tariff of 1930, which Bhagwati in the above quote portrays as a radical departure from a historic free-trade stance, only marginally (if at all) increased the degree of protectionism in the U.S. economy. [The] average tariff rate for manufactured goods that resulted from this bill was 48%, and it still falls within the range of the average rates that had prevailed in the United States since the Civil War, albeit in the upper region of this range. It is only in relation to the brief "liberal" interlude of 1913–1929 that the 1930 tariff bill can be interpreted as increasing protectionism, although even then it was not by very much (from 37% in 1925 to 48% in 1931, [...]).

In this context, it is also important to note that the American Civil War was fought on the issue of tariffs as much as, if not more than, on the issue of slavery. Of the two major issues that divided the North and the South, the South had actually more to fear on the tariff front than on the slavery front. Abraham Lincoln was a well-known protectionist who had cut his political teeth under the charismatic politician Henry Clay in the Whig Party, which advocated the "American System" based on infrastructural development and protectionism, thus recognizing that free trade was in the "British" interest (Luthin, 1944, pp. 610–11; Frayssé, 1986, pp. 99–100). Moreover, Lincoln thought the blacks were racially inferior and slave emancipation was an idealistic proposal with no prospect of immediate implementation (Garraty & Carnes, 2000, pp. 391–92; Foner, 1998, p. 92). He is said to have emancipated the slaves in 1862 as a strategic move to win the war rather than out of some moral conviction (Garraty & Carnes, 2000, p. 405).

It was only after the Second World War, with its industrial supremacy unchallenged, that the U.S. liberalized its trade (although not as unequivocally as Britain did in the mid-nineteenth century) and started championing the cause of free trade—once again proving List right on his "ladder kicking" metaphor. The following quote from Ulysses Grant, the Civil War hero and president of the United States from 1868 to 1876 clearly shows how the Americans had no illusions about ladder-kicking on the British side and their side.

"For centuries England has relied on protection, has carried it to extremes and has obtained satisfactory results from it. There is no doubt that it is to this system that it owes its present strength. After two centuries, England has found it convenient to adopt free trade because it thinks that protection can no longer offer it anything. Very well then, Gentlemen, my knowledge of our country leads me to believe that within 200 years, when America has gotten out of protection all that it can offer, it too will adopt free trade." (Ulysses S. Grant, president of the United States, 1868–1876, cited in A.G. Frank, *Capitalism and Underdevelopment in Latin America*, New York, Monthly Review Press, 1967, p. 164).

Important as it may have been, tariff protection was not the only policy deployed by the U.S. government in order to promote the country's economic development during its catch-up phase. At least from the 1830s, it supported an extensive range of agricultural research through the granting of government land to agricultural colleges and the establishment of government research institutes (Kozul-Wright, 1995, p. 100). In the second half of the nineteenth century, it expanded public educational investments—in 1840, less than half of the total investment in education was public, whereas by 1900 this figure had risen to almost 80%—and raised the literacy ratio to 94% by 1900 (p. 101, especially f.n. 37). It also promoted the development of transportation infrastructure, especially through the granting of land and subsidies to railway companies (pp. 101–102).

And it is important to recognize that the role of the U.S. federal government in industrial development has been substantial even in the post-war era, thanks to the large amount of defense-related procurements and research and development (R&D) spending, which have had enormous spillover effects (Shapiro & Taylor, 1990, p. 866; Owen, 1966, ch. 9; Mowery & Rosenberg, 1993). The share of the U.S. federal government in total R&D spending, which was only 16% in 1930 (Owen, 1966, pp. 149–50), remained between one-half and two-thirds during the postwar years

(Mowery & Rosenberg, 1993, table 2.3). The critical role of the U.S. government's National Institutes of Health (NIH) in supporting R&D in pharmaceutical and biotechnology industries should also be mentioned. Even according to the U.S. pharmaceutical industry association itself (see http://www.phrma.org/publications), only 43% of pharmaceutical R&D is funded by the industry itself, while 29% is funded by the NIH.

GERMANY

Germany is a country that is today commonly known as the home of infant industry protection, both intellectually and in terms of policies. However, historically speaking, tariff protection actually played a much less important role in the economic development of Germany than that of Britain or the United States .

The tariff protection for industry in Prussia before the 1834 German customs union under its leadership (*Zollverein*), and that subsequently accorded to German industry in general remained mild (Blackbourn, 1997, p. 117). In 1879, the Chancellor of Germany, Otto von Bismarck introduced a great tariff increase in order to cement the political alliance between the *Junkers* (landlords) and the heavy industrialists–the so-called "marriage of iron and rye." However, even after this, substantial protection was accorded only to the key heavy industries, especially the iron and steel industry, and industrial protection in general remained low (Blackbourn, 1997, p. 320). [The] level of protection in German manufacturing was one of the *lowest* among comparable countries throughout the nineteenth century and the first half of the twentieth century.

The relatively low tariff protection does not, however, mean that the German state took a *laissez-faire* approach to economic development. Especially under Frederick William I (1713–1740) and Frederick the Great (1740–1786) in the eighteenth century, the Prussian state pursued a range of policies to promote new industries–especially textiles (linen above all), metals, armaments, porcelain, silk, and sugar refining–by providing monopoly rights, trade protection, export subsidies, capital investments, and skilled workers from abroad (Trebilcock, 1981, pp. 136–52).

From the early nineteenth century, the Prussian state also invested in infrastructure–the most famous example being the government financing of road building in the Ruhr (Milward & Saul, 1979, p. 417). It also implemented educational reform, which not only involved building new schools and universities but also the re-orientation of their teaching from theology to science and technology–this at a time when science and technology was not taught in Oxford or Cambridge (Kindleberger, 1978, p. 191).

There were some growth-retarding effects of Prussian government intervention, such as the opposition to the development of banking (Kindleberger, 1978, pp. 199–200). However, on the whole, we cannot but agree with the statement by Milward & Saul (1979) that "[t]o successive industrialising countries the attitude taken by early nineteenth-century German governments seemed much more nearly in touch with economic realities than the rather idealised and frequently simplified model of what had happened in Britain or France which economists presented to them" (p. 418).

After the 1840s, with the growth of the private sector, the involvement of the German state in industrial development became less pronounced (Trebilcock, 1981, p. 77). However, this did not mean a withdrawal of the state, rather a transition from a directive to a guiding role. During the Second Reich (1870–1914), there was further erosion in state capacity and involvement in relation to industrial development, although it still played an important role through its tariff policy and cartel policy (Tilly, 1996).

FRANCE

Similar to the case of Germany, there is an enduring myth about French economic policy. This is the view, propagated mainly by British liberal opinion, that France has always been a state-led economy, kind of an anti-thesis to *laissez-faire* Britain. This characterization may largely apply to the pre-Revolutionary period and to the post-World War II period in the country's history, but not to the rest of it.

French economic policy in the pre-Revolutionary period—often known as *Colbertism*, named after Jean-Baptiste Colbert (1619–1683), the famous finance minister under Louis XIV—was certainly highly interventionist. For example, in the early eighteenth century, the French state tried to recruit skilled workers from Britain on a large scale and encouraged industrial espionage.

The Revolution, however, significantly upset this course. Milward & Saul (1979) argue that the Revolution brought about a marked shift in French government economic policy, because "the destruction of absolutism seemed connected in the minds of the revolutionaries with the introduction of a more *laissez-faire* system" (p. 284). Especially after the fall of Napoleon, the *laissez-faire* policy regime got firmly established and persisted until the Second World War.

For example, challenging the conventional wisdom that pitches free-trade Britain against protectionist France during the nineteenth century, Nye (1991) examines detailed empirical evidence and concludes that "France's trade regime was more liberal than that of Great Britain throughout most of the nineteenth century, even in the period from 1840 to 1860 [the alleged beginning of full-fledged free trade in Britain]" (p. 25). [When] measured by net customs revenue as a percentage of net import values (which is a standard measure of protectionism, especially among the historians), France was always less protectionist than Britain between 1821 and 1875, and especially until the early 1860s.

What is interesting to note is that the partial exception to this century and a half period of "liberalism" in France under Napoleon III (1848–1870) was the only period of economic dynamism in France during this period (Trebilcock, 1981, p. 184). Under Napoleon III, the French state actively encouraged infrastructural developments and established various institutions of research and teaching (Bury, 1964, ch. 4). It also modernized the country's financial sector by granting limited liability to, investing in, and overseeing modern large-scale financial institutions (Cameron, 1953).

On the trade policy front, Napoleon III signed the famous Anglo-French trade treaty (the Cobden-Chevalier treaty) of 1860, which heralded the period of trade liberalism on the Continent (1860–1879) (see Kindleberger, 1975, for further details). However [...] the degree of protectionism in France was already quite low on the eve of the treaty (it was actually lower than in Britain at the time), and therefore the resulting reduction in protectionism was relatively small.

The treaty was allowed to lapse in 1892 and many tariff rates, especially ones on manufacturing, were raised. However, this had little positive effects of the kind that we saw in the similar move in countries like Sweden at the time [...] because there was no coherent industrial upgrading strategy behind this tariff increase. Especially during the Third Republic, the French government was almost as *laissez-faire* in its attitude towards economic matters as the then very *laissez-faire* British government (Kuisel, 1981, pp. 12–13).

It was only after the Second World War that the French elite got galvanized into re-organizing their state machinery in order to address the problem of the country's (relative) industrial backwardness. During this time, especially until the late 1960s, the French state used indicative planning, state-owned enterprises, and what is now somewhat misleadingly known as "East-Asian-style" industrial policy in order to catch up with the more advanced countries. As a result, France witnessed a very successful structural transformation of its economy, and finally overtook Britain (see Shonfield, 1965 and Hall, 1986).

SWEDEN

Sweden did not enter its modern age with a free trade regime. After the end of the Napoleonic wars, its government enacted a strongly protective tariff law (1816), and banned the imports and exports of some items (Gustavson, 1986, p. 15). However, from about 1830 on, protection was progressively lowered (p. 65), and in 1857, a very low tariff regime was introduced (Bohlin, 1999, p. 155; […]).

This free trade phase, however, was short-lived. Sweden started using tariffs as a means to protect the agricultural sector from American competition since around 1880. After 1892, it also provided tariff protection and subsidies to the industrial sector, especially the newly-emerging engineering sector (Chang & Kozul-Wright, 1994, p. 869; Bohlin, 1999, p. 156). Because of this switch to protectionism, the Swedish economy performed extremely well in the following decades. According to a calculation by Baumol et al. (1990), Sweden was, after Finland, the second fastest growing (in terms of GDP per work-hour) of the sixteen major industrial economies between 1890 and 1900, and the fastest growing between 1900 and 1913 (p. 88, table 5.1).

Tariff protection and subsidies were not all that Sweden used in order to promote industrial development. More interestingly, during the late nineteenth century, Sweden developed a tradition of close public-private coop-eration to the extent that was difficult to find parallel in other countries at the time, including Germany with its long tradi-tion of public-private partnership. This first developed out of state involvement in the agricultural irrigation and drainage schemes (Samuelsson, 1968, pp. 71–76). This was then applied to the development of railways from the 1850s, tele-graph and telephone in the 1880s, and hydro-electric energy in the 1890s (Chang & Kozul-Wright, 1994, pp. 869–70; Bohlin, 1999, pp. 153–55). Public-private collaboration also existed in certain key industries, such as the iron industry (Gustavson, 1986, pp. 71–72; Chang & Kozul-Wright, 1994, p. 870). Inter-estingly, all these resemble the patterns of public-private collaboration for which the East Asian economies later became famous (Evans, 1995, is a classic work on this issue).

The Swedish state made great efforts in facilitating the acquisition of advanced foreign technology, including state-sponsored industrial espionage. However, more notable was its emphasis on the accumulation of "technological capabilities" (see Fransman & King (eds.), 1984, and Lall, 1992, for pioneering works on this issue). It provided stipends and travel grants for studies and research, invested in education, helped the establishment of technological research institutes, and provided direct research funding to industry (Chang & Kozul-Wright, 1994, p. 870).

Swedish economic policy underwent a significant change after the electoral victory of the Socialist Party in 1932 (which has been out of the office for less than ten years since then) and the signing of the "historical pact" between the union and the employers' association in 1936 (the *Saltsjöbaden* agreement) (see Korpi, 1983). The policy regime that emerged after the 1936 pact initially focused on the construction of a system where the employers will finance a generous welfare state and high investment in return for wage moderation from the union.

After the Second World War, use was made of the regime's potential for promoting industrial upgrading. In the 1950s and the 1960s, the centralized trade union, LO (*Landsorganisationen i Sverige*) adopted the so-called Rehn-Meidner Plan (LO, 1963, is the document that set out the strategy in detail). This introduced the so-called solidaristic wage policy, which explicitly aimed to equalize wages across industries for the same types of workers. It was expected that this would generate pressure on the capitalists in low-wage sectors to upgrade their capital stock or shed labor, while allowing the capitalists in the high-wage sector to retain extra profits and expand faster than it would otherwise have been possible. This was complemented by the so-called active labor market policy, which provided retraining and relocation supports to the workers displaced in this process of industrial upgrading. It is widely accepted that this strategy contributed to Sweden's successful industrial upgrading in the early post-war years (Edquist & Lundvall, 1993, p. 274).

THE NETHERLANDS

The Netherlands was, as it is well known, the world's dominant naval and commercial powers during the seventeenth century, its so-called "Golden Century," thanks to its aggressive "mercantilist" regulations on navigation, fishing, and international trade since the sixteenth century. However, it showed a marked decline in the eighteenth century, the so-called "Periwig Period" (*Pruikentijd*), with its defeat in the 1780 Fourth Anglo-Dutch War marking the symbolic end to its international supremacy (Boxer, 1965, ch. 10).

A policy paralysis seems to have gripped the Netherlands between the late seventeenth century and the early twentieth century. The only exception to this was the effort by King William I (1815–1840), who established many agencies providing subsidized industrial financing (Kossmann, 1978, pp. 136–38; van Zanden, 1996, pp. 84–85). He also strongly supported the development of a modern cotton textile industry, especially in the Twente region (Henderson, 1972, pp. 198–200).

However, from the late 1840s, the country reverted to a *laissez-faire* regime, which lasted until the Second World War. [Excerpt] for Britain in the late nineteenth century, and Japan before the restoration of tariff autonomy, the Netherlands remained the least protected economy among the NDCs. Also, the country abolished the patent law (which was first introduced in 1817) in 1869, inspired by the anti-patent movement that swept Europe at the time, which condemned patent as just another form of monopoly (Schiff, 1971, Machlup & Penrose, 1950). Despite international pressures, the country refused to re-introduce the patent law until 1912.

On the whole, during this extreme *laissez-faire* period, the Dutch economy remained rather sluggish, and its industrialization remained relatively shallow. According to the authoritative estimate by Maddison (1995), measured in 1990 dollars, it was the second richest country in the world even after Britain in 1820, even after a century of relative decline ($1,756 vs. $1,561). However, a century later (1913), it was overtaken by no less than six countries–Australia, New Zealand, the United States, Canada, Switzerland, and Belgium–and almost by Germany.

It was largely for this reason that the end of World War II saw the introduction of more interventionist policies (van Zanden, 1999, pp. 182–84). Especially up to 1963, rather active trade and industrial policies were practised. These included: financial supports for two large firms (one in steel, the other in soda); subsidies to industrialize backward areas; encouragement of technical education; encouraging the development of the aluminium industry through subsidized gas; and the development of key infrastructures.

SWITZERLAND

Switzerland was one of the earliest industrializers of Europe–starting its Industrial Revolution barely twenty years later than Britain (Biucchi, 1973, p. 628). It was a world technological leader in a number of important industries (Milward & Saul, 1979, pp. 454–55), especially in the cotton textile industry, where it was deemed technologically more advanced in many areas than Britain (Biucchi, 1973, p. 629).

Given this very small (if at all) technological gap with the leader country, infant industry protection was not necessary for Switzerland. Also, given its small size, protection would have been more costly for the country than would have been the case for bigger countries. Moreover, given its highly decentralized political structure and very small size, there was little room for centralized infant industry protection (Biucchi, 1973, p. 455).

However, Switzerland's *laissez-faire* trade policy did not mean that its government had no sense of strategy in its policy-making. Its refusal to introduce a patent law until 1907, despite strong international pressure, is such an example. This anti-patent policy is argued to have contributed to the country's development–especially by allowing the "theft" of German ideas in the chemical and pharmaceutical industries and by encouraging foreign direct investments in the food industry (see Schiff, 1971, and Chang, 2001).

JAPAN AND THE EAST ASIAN NEWLY INDUSTRIALIZED COUNTRIES

Soon after it was forced open by the Americans in 1853, Japan 's feudal political order collapsed and a modernizing regime was established after the so-called Meiji Restoration of 1868. The role of the state since then has been crucial in the country's development.

Until 1911, Japan was *not* able to use tariff protection, due to the "unequal treaties" that barred it from having tariff rates over 5%. Therefore, the Japanese state had to use other means to encourage industrialization. To start with, it established state-owned "model factories" (or "pilot plants") in a number of industries—notably in shipbuilding, mining, textile, and military industries (Smith, 1955, and Allen, 1981). Although most of these were privatized by the 1870s, it continued to subsidize the privatized firms, especially in shipbuilding (McPherson, 1987, p. 31, pp. 34–35). Subsequently, it established the first modern steel mill, and developed railways and telegraph (McPherson, 1987, p. 31; Smith, 1955, pp. 44–45).

Following the ending of the unequal treaties in 1911, the Japanese state started introducing a range of tariff reforms intended to protect infant industries, make imported raw materials more affordable, and control the imports of luxury consumption goods (McPherson, 1987, p. 32). During the 1920s, under strong German influence (Johnson, 1982, pp. 105–106), it started encouraging "rationalization" of key industries by sanctioning cartel arrangements and encouraging mergers, which were aimed at restraining "wasteful competition," achieving scale economies, standardization, and the introduction of scientific management (McPherson,

1987, pp. 32–33). These efforts were intensified in the 1930s (Johnson, 1982, pp. 105–115).

Despite all these developmental efforts, during the first half of the twentieth century, Japan was on the whole *not* the economic superstar that it became after World War II. According to Maddison (1989), between 1900 and 1950, Japan 's per capita income growth rate was only 1% p.a.. This was somewhat below the average for the sixteen largest NDCs that he studied, which was 1.3% p.a., although it must be noted that part of this rather poor performance was due to the dramatic collapse in output following defeat in the Second World War.

Between the end of World War II and the early 1970s, Japan's growth record was unrivalled. According to the data from Maddison (1989, p. 35, Table 3.2), between 1950 and 1973, per capita GDP in Japan grew at a staggering 8%, more than double the 3.8% average achieved by the sixteen NDCs mentioned above (the average includes Japan). The next best performers among the NDCs were Germany, Austria (both at 4.9%) and Italy (4.8%), while even the East Asian "miracle" developing countries like Taiwan (6.2%) or Korea (5.2%) came nowhere near Japan, despite the bigger "convergence" effect that they could expect given their greater economic backwardness.

In the economic successes of Japan and other East Asian countries (except Hong Kong), interventionist trade and industrial policies played a crucial role. Notable are the similarities between their policies and those used by other NDCs before them, including, above all, eighteenth-century Britain and nineteenth-century United States. However, it is also important to note that the policies used by the East Asian countries (and indeed those used by some other NDCs, like France) during the postwar period were a lot more sophisticated and fine-tuned than their historical equivalents.

They used more substantial and better-designed export subsidies (both direct and indirect) and much less export taxes than in the earlier experiences (Luedde-Neurath, 1986; Amsden, 1989). Tariff rebates for imported raw materials and machinery for export industries were much more systematically used than in, for example, eighteenth-century Britain (Lueede-Neurath, 1986).

Coordination of complementary investments, which had been previously done in a rather haphazard way (if at all), was systematized through indicative planning and government investment programs (Chang, 1993 and 1994). Regulations of firm entry, exit, investments, and pricing intended to "manage competition" were a lot more aware of the dangers of monopolistic abuses and more sensitive to its impact on export market performance, when compared to their historical counterparts, namely, the late nineteenth and early twentieth-century cartel policies (Amsden & Singh, 1994; Chang, forthcoming).

The East Asian states also integrated human capital and learning-related policies into their industrial policy framework more tightly than their predecessors had done, through "manpower planning" (You & Chang, 1993). Regulations on technology licensing and foreign direct investments were much more sophisticated and comprehensive than in the earlier experiences (Chang, 1998). Subsidies to (and public provision of) education, training, and R&D were also much more systematic and extensive than their historical counterparts (Lall & Teubal, 1998).

1. How did free trade develop differently around the world? What were some of the reasons countries adopted free trade agreements?

2. What role did the Smoot-Hawley Act play in developing free trade agreements in the United States?

"WAS 2016 THE YEAR THE WORLD TURNED ITS BACK ON FREE TRADE?" BY JULIEN CHAISSE AND QIAN WANG, FROM *THE CONVERSATION*, JANUARY 16, 2017

Fear of and misunderstanding about free trade and globalisation brought us a turbulent 2016. And the last few months have been a wake-up call about the dramatic slowdown in international trade, presaging a major change in global policies.

In its September forecast, the World Trade Organization (WTO) warned that it was worried world trade would only grow by 1.7% (in volume) in 2016. This is its lowest growth since 2009, the year of the global financial crisis, when international trade started retreating.

Worse still is the phenomenon of international trade growing at a slightly slower pace than global production.

The ratio of international trade-to-GDP, which indicates the relative importance of international trade in the economy of a country, has been falling sharply since 2009 except a gradual recovery in 2010-2011.

According to the October 2016 IMF World Economic Outlook, international trade in goods and services has grown at the mediocre rate of around 3% a year since 2012, less than half of the growth of the previous three decades. Between 1985 and 2007, world trade increased, on average, twice as fast as world production, whereas for the past four years it has just kept pace.

This is an historic change. If the WTO forecast for 2016 were to be confirmed, world trade would have risen less rapidly than world GDP, which grew between 2.2% and 2.9% in the first half of 2016.

THE END OF GLOBALISATION?

This could indeed be evidence for the beginning of globalisation going in reverse. The globalisation of trade means that countries trade more and more with each other, and that trade between them increases faster than their national production.

Has globalisation, which is the modern form of the international division of labour, reached its peak? Those good old times when companies, mainly multinationals, achieve production efficiency and generated more revenue through outsourcing their labour-intensive work abroad than manufacturing at home.

The IMF suggests three explanations for the decline in trade regimes: the slowdown in global economic growth; the halt in trade and investment liberalisation agreements (which started long before the freezing of the Trans Pacific Partnership or the Trans Atlantic Trade and Partnership agreements); and the maturity of international production chains that would have exhausted their advantages.

Geopolitical competition in global trade agenda-setting among the US, the European Union and emerging powers, such as China and India, and increasingly popular protectionism rhetoric in national trade debates also explain the failure or lack of cooperation in the multilateral trading system.

THREE TYPES OF EXPLANATIONS

IMF experts estimate that the slowdown in economic growth since 2012, after the temporary catch up in 2010 and 2011, explains by itself "about three-quarters of the dramatic slowdown trade".

Proof of this, they argue, is that it's investment products, and secondarily, durable household goods, such as cars, whose trade has slowed down the most. They note that slowdown of goods consumption affects 143 countries out of 171 under review, including China, Brazil and the nations in the Euro area, among others.

In this respect, the period between 2012 and 2016 will have been particularly volatile in terms of world trade, resulting from the collapse of oil and commodity prices. The IMF notes that this fall itself resulted in a 10.5%

contraction of all international trade in 2015, when looking at all products.

This has resulted in considerable loss of purchasing power for many countries and billions of consumers, and thus a reorientation of demand at the expense of durable goods, which have become inaccessible to many. Added to this are national trade imbalances – the surpluses of some countries and the deficits of others – that have also acted as a brake on trade.

The second explanation for shrinking international trade stems from the general global climate, which has become more protectionist. The IMF notes that, in the 1990s, an average of 30 trade liberalisation agreements were signed annually between countries. But barely ten such agreements have been signed each year since 2011.

Free trade agreements include deeper provisions that go beyond trade barriers and more partners can significantly reduce the cost of trade, which, in turn, helps boost trade flows.

The third reason for the brake on trade is the decline in the growth of global value chains, which is the idea that the process of production consists of many stages and occurs across borders. But this phenomenon, which developed at a very high rate after China's accession to the WTO in 2001 as the country emerged as a global supplier, has now reached cruising pace.

Similarly, the fall in the cost of cross-border transportation and international cost of telecommunications, which had contributed so much to trade, would also have met its limit. And they probably contribute modestly to the decline of global trade.

But even as they worry about the disappointing numbers, countries remain very divided on what to do next. In fact, we may be witnessing the return of an economic nationalism that threatens withdrawal from the global market.

PROSPECTS FOR 2017

It seems, then, that the only diagnosis is that the global economy is slowing down and the risks to recovery are picking up. Challenges range from Brexit to the slowdown in emerging markets, from the collapse of commodity prices to rising geopolitical tensions.

Part of the problem is that the level of public debt of countries is too high for them to have significant room for manoeuvre. And countries that have the means, such as Germany, refuse to spend more.

At least, in the last months of 2016 the G20 leaders' communique recognised the impact excess capacity has had on the global economy and there's now a chance of focusing on this problem. Excess global capacity in steel and other industries is mainly a result of falling demand, rising production and excessive government subsidies.

The impact of the crisis has been so severe on market demand that all G20 leaders are turning to overcapacity, following the example of China. Until current overcapacity is absorbed, the recovery will be slow.

But the remedy has the social cost of job loss, and that could fuel the already high risk in the United States and Europe of fragmented national politics.

On the bright side is the noteworthy G20 Guiding Principle for Global Investment Policymaking reached under Chinese presidency and endorsed by G20 heads of state. It lays out a roadmap for future investment policy and the correlation between investment and sustainable development.

In the 19th century, debates over drivers of economic growth—tariffs or free trade—dominated the political scene. Mercifully, the idea of free trade has persisted but it now faces serious challenges.

It seems that, at best, 2017 will be another difficult year. The most we may be able to hope for is that national trade-restriction measures will be compatible with WTO rules.

In any event, we have not finished paying for the consequences of the financial crisis. If history is any indication, trade deals, which are always better in the multilateral format (such as under the WTO), are the world's best hope for avoiding another global recession.

1. According to the author, why are people turning away from free trade?

2. What changes in the global economy have brought about these changes?

"THE IMPACT OF INTERNATIONAL FREE-TRADE AGREEMENTS ON JOB GROWTH AND PROSPERITY," BY HARLEY SHAIKEN, FROM *JOURNALIST'S RESOURCE*, JANUARY 15, 2015

As the U.S. Congress debates whether to expedite another round of major international trade agreements, what do we know about how similar pacts worked out in the past? Twenty one years after its start in 1994, the North American Free Trade Agreement (NAFTA) offers the best evidence we have. This pact among the United States, Canada and Mexico created the world's largest free-trade area and has been unquestionably successful in expanding cross-border commerce. Over two decades from 1993 to 2013, total merchandise trades between the United States and Mexico increased almost six-fold—from $80 billion to $459 billion.

But expanded trade was not an end in itself. Trade growth was supposed to generate new jobs, lift incomes and stimulate economic development. Unfortunately, research shows that twenty years of expanded trade between the United States and Mexico has produced disappointing results for the larger goals that count. The North American Free Trade Agreement stands as a cautionary tale about what could unfold after similar pacts to further unleash global trade.

SUCCESSFUL TRADE EXPANSION WITHOUT PROJECTED BENEFITS

As part of his effort to persuade Congress to pass the North American Free Trade agreement in 1993, President

Bill Clinton predicted that exports from the United States to Mexico would boom, generating a million U.S. jobs in five years. Backing up Clinton's claim about American job growth, supportive economists predicted a trade surplus for the United States in its dealings with Mexico—that is, they estimated that U.S. exports were projected to exceed its imports from Mexico.

Unfortunately, these optimistic predictions were not borne out—U.S. trade with Mexico went from a slight surplus in 1994 to an almost $100 billion deficit in 2013. As a result of this trade imbalance, the Economic Policy Institute estimates that instead of the million new jobs that President Clinton promised, 700,000 U.S. workers ended up being displaced.

For Mexico, the results seem at first glance to be more positive. The expansion of exports to the United States has stimulated the growth of more advanced manufacturing technologies and led to the creation of new jobs in export manufacturing. However, a closer look at the effects of the North American pact on the Mexican economy reveals a less positive story, because as Mexico's trade surplus with the U.S. has grown, its trade deficit with China has exploded. These two trends have unfolded together because almost three-fourths of Mexico's manufactured exports to the United States are products assembled from imported parts and components. Only three percent of the exports from Mexican border plants are assembled from sources within Mexico.

For Mexico and the United States alike, in short, trade expansion has been only weakly connected to domestic economic growth, a disturbing fact given all the rosy promises at the time the North American Free Trade Agreement was instituted.

RISING PRODUCTIVITY AND DECLINING WAGES

As the United States and Mexico share expanded trade across their border, both countries have also experienced a waning connection between trends in economic productivity and wages. Productivity has gone up as trade has expanded, but wages have stagnated or even declined.

By 2011, productivity in the United States had risen to about 170% of what it was when the North American Free Trade Agreement was instituted. But the average U.S. worker has not reaped much benefit from this improvement in the productivity of the economy. Real hourly compensation for American workers rose by only about 16% in the same period.

In Mexico, the relationship has been even more disappointing. By the time the North American trade agreement was implemented in 1994, Mexican manufacturing wages had been declining for more than a decade — they were 30% below what they had been in 1980. To counter domestic opposition to the agreement, Mexican politicians relied heavily on claims that more trade with the United States would reverse the prior wage deterioration.

We now know that, like President Clinton's promises about job creation, the arguments from Mexican trade supporters were based on the false assumption that trade expansion would automatically lead to rising wages. Expanded trade certainly helped stimulate new investment, and the adoption of more advanced manufacturing technologies in Mexico helped, in turn, to generate increases in productivity. Labor productivity in Mexican manufacturing rose by 76% between 1994 and 2011. However, when adjusted for inflation, typical hourly compensation for Mexican manufacturing workers did not improve. As a matter of fact, in 2011 wage compensation was 20% below what it was at the start of the North American Free Trade Agreement—not at all what had been projected by boosters of the pact.

CAUTIONARY LESSONS FROM THE PAST

What can we learn from this historical experience? The most important lesson is straightforward: trade expansion should not become an end in itself. In all countries that are party to possible pacts, the real stakes for citizens lie in more and better jobs, in economic growth that benefits most workers and families. Experience with the North American Free Trade Agreement shows that trade may very well grow without spurring more jobs or ensuring shared prosperity. Proponents of unleashing ever more trade across borders invariably claim that new pacts will "lift all boats," helping workers on both sides of the border. But the record shows that such rosy thinking was misplaced for the North American Free Trade Agreement. Now, the same misplaced optimism may be in play again. Rather than rush into new rounds of disappointing decisions to vastly expand global trade, Americans need to be sure their elected legislators support only the kinds of international agreements that truly encourage prosperity for all.

1. What is the relationship between free trade and economic growth?

2. In your opinion, how can trade agreements address the issues raised by the author?

EXCERPT FROM "GLOBALIZATION, GOVERNANCE, DEMOCRATIZATION AND FAIR TRADE," BY RASTO OVIN AND PEDJA AŠANIN GOLE, FROM *INTECH*, FEBRUARY 1, 2017

1. INTRODUCTION

Although being an element of sustainable economics—related to regional policy—fair trade has been discussed and explained primarily from the position of civilization development goals and is subject to mainly soft approach of governance. It is, of course, the role of progressive individuals and NGOs to point to the areas, which should enter mainstream government policies' perspectives. On the other hand, however, the ability to act for the solution of the problem is not on the side of such pluralist approach. These are governments of leading economies, who should adopt principles of fair trade, as they are in the line of the contemporary level of civilization as well as a must for creation of sustainable global trade environment. Unlike partial knowledge and perspective of individual fair trade promoters, the governments dispose of overbroad and direct access to information, resources and tools to act in support of fair trade.

With the help of comparative approach in this chapter, we are pointing to the fact that fair trade is a necessary route to make international trade sustainable, and we are trying to explain why it will remain the competence and responsibility of governments in industrial economies. The main argument of this chapter is that present fair trade initiatives lack fundaments of economics as well as of the theory of economic policy. While the first one requires much broader definition and impact of the fair trade, the second poses inevitable requirements for the level that can make this concept work.

2. ECONOMICS OF FAIR TRADE

The basic principle of regional policy is that underdeveloped regions will get the opportunity to catch up with the developed regions when (if) there will be trade among them. Deepening of trade relations will help to engage underdeveloped regions in economic areas together with industrial economies. Including this principle means to automatically exclude the trade based on exploration of undeveloped regions' resources and to include the sustainability principle. The sustainability risk of such 'unfair trade' for developed economies appears in three forms. The first one is that oppression of trade partners and prices of exporters to industrial economies leads to cost and price competition that at the end cannot be sustained by developed economies themselves. The second one refers to the need of transfer campaigns to help underdeveloped regions (states). They usually serve only for the pacification of certain states or groups that threaten to bring destruction to established trade and security context. The third form has been demonstrated with recent immigration developments in the EU. According to European Commission Vice President Frans Timmermans [1], it is assessed that 60% of immigrants are moving for economic reasons—thus it is not difficult to recognize the pattern, which may prevail if the population's perspective in low-income countries will not develop.

It has not been proved anything else that humans react to economic stimulations in a pattern that partially resembles laws of physics. Here it is enough to mention the laws on prices and quantities of supply and demand. It is, however, a requirement of civilization stance and sustainability as discussed above to promote institutional arrangements for assuring opportunities for states and groups, who were deprived of their political and economic development.

3. FAIR TRADE TERMINOLOGY AND PRESENT DEVELOPMENTS

The term "fair trade" is a generic concept. The World Fair Trade Organization as a global network of fair trade organizations defines fair trade as "a trading partnership, based on dialogue, transparency and respect, which seeks greater equity in international trade. It contributes to sustainable development by offering better trading conditions to, and securing the rights of, marginalised producers and workers, especially in the South. Fair Trade Organizations (backed by consumers) are engaged actively in supporting producers, awareness raising and in campaigning for changes in the rules and practice of conventional international trade [2, 3]."

Fair trade is also an international movement to socially regulate global markets (particularly in the food sector) who seeks to empower producers in the global South (through the provision of better prices, stable market links and development resources) and to promote responsible consumption and provide shoppers with socially and environmentally friendly products in the global

North. This movement is therefore a favour of social and environmental justice and develops alternative economic spaces of production, trade, retailing and consumption. According to Encyclopedia of Political Theory [4], "the goals of the fair trade movement include improving the livelihoods and well-being of small producers; promoting development opportunities for disadvantaged groups of producers, in particular women and indigenous people; raising awareness among consumers of the negative effects of patterns of international trade on producers in the Global South; campaigning for changes in the regulatory regimes governing international trade; and the protection and promotion of human rights. The international fair trade movement consists of certification agencies, producer organizations and cooperatives, trading networks, and retailers."

The explanation of the term "fair trade" by the Fairtrade Foundation reads: "With fair trade you have the power to change the world every day. With simple shopping choices, you can get farmers a better deal. And that means they can make their own decisions, control their futures and lead the dignified life everyone deserves [5]." Such explanation is not only normative but is also vague and is subject to historical anthropomorphism to such extent that it cannot be used for economic analysis.

Somewhat clearer is the description of fair trade as "organized social movement and market—based approach that aims to help producers in developing countries to make better trading conditions and promote sustainability. The movement advocates the payment of higher prices to exporters as well as higher social and environmental standards. It focuses in particular on exports from developing countries to develop countries, most notably handicrafts, coffee, cocoa, sugar, tea, bananas, honey, cotton, wine, fresh fruit, chocolate, flowers and gold [6, 7]." Basing on the role of trade in reducing regional differences, we believe that the established concept of fair trade as presented above is simple to narrow. If we recognize the ricochet effects of unfair trade for developed economies, we simply should understand fair trade as an element of sustainable trade and of economics in a broader sense.

Therefore, we are underlining our disagreement with the interpretation that the fair trade concept refers only to developing economies and regions. It is a minimum requirement to see a broad picture, where disequilibria in global trade are taking us in the era of almost unlimited mobility of information and resources. Therefore, the concept of fair trade has to do with the sustainability of trade and development in industrial economies as well as on the global level. Despite our rejection of criticism over globalization, here we have to point to the unfairness of trade that is felt on the side of industrial countries. It is the fact that inhuman exploration of resources in low-income countries may lead to price competition that cannot be followed by any economy following basic human rights and environmental principles. Here again, we come to a bend, where promoting fair trade is in the interest of industrial economies themselves.

In this respect, one should understand the rejection of globalism by numerous political leaders in the West. Not only are developed economies "threatening" jobs in developed country, even the critics of Trade and Investment Partnership between the EU and USA partially point to the risk of losing jobs on both sides of Atlantic. Initiatives worrying about job preservation as, for instance, Campaign for America's future are quite specific about the risk of the TPP. In their communication from August 12, 2016, they line up behind the warning by former US presidency Democratic candidate Sanders, stating that "[The Obama administration] continue pushing forward on the disastrous Trans-Pacific Partnership trade agreement that will cost American jobs, harm the environment, increase the cost of prescription drugs and threaten our ability to protect public health [8]." The fact that this initiative considers itself as a fair trade movement only supports our above-presented perspective of a developed economy.

4. GLOBALIZATION: FROM "FREE TRADE" TO "FAIR TRADE"

Globalization stems from a basic human need to seek a better and more fulfilling life. Starting from such defi-nition of globalization, we can say that it is the faithful companion of human's spiritual, economic and political development but also the expression of transportation and communication opportunities. Today globalization processes of the liberalization of [...] trade grew out of Bretton Woods Conference in 1944 [...] establishing three important international institutions, in which the function is the foundation of the existence of relatively autono-mous, state-regulated national economies [...]: (1) the International Bank of Reconstruction and Development (IBRD, more commonly known as the World Bank); (2) the International Monetary Fund (IMF), the dollar-based gold exchange currency system; and (3) the General Agree-ment on Trade and Tariffs (GATT). These institutions proclaim and spread the "free trade," "free markets" and increasingly unrestricted access to a wide range of markets to transnational corporations.

[The] GATT came into existence in 1947 as part of a plan for general economic recovery after the Second World War. Then globalization discussions were carried out to remove the barriers to free trade under the GATT umbrella. The GATT's main purpose was to reduce barriers to international trade and it operated until 1994. Following the dissolution of the Cold War, the idea of globalization came to prominence, and in 1995 the GATT was replaced by the World Trade Organization (WTO). The WTO has promoted and developed the institutional foundations for "free trade" as the important implications on the modes of production: free movement of goods and services together with the free movement of capital but not the free movement of labour.

Many authors locate globalization within economic phenomena and more specifically within the chain of production, trade and finance. As noted by Rosamond, '"[f]or some, globalization simply refers to dramatically increased volumes in international trade. For others, globalization is better thought of as global economic integration, [...] cross-border flows of capital, goods, labour, and firms who creating genuinely global markets, which in turn accentuate the permeability of national economic borders [9]." It is about the economistic definitions of globalization and possibilities for economic governance. In a globalized world and transnational economic space, sovereign governments are losing the capacity to exercise effective economic governance over their own national jurisdictions, and their raison d'être becomes the adjustment of the domestic political economy to imperatives of powerful non-state forces that dominate the contemporary global economy.

The origin of the globalization movement was assumed to provide a framework for global equality and integration [10]. But very soon the globalization movement acquired a bad reputation: opposite globalization calls for a "free trade" of goods and services has raised anti-globalism movement with the requirements of "fair trade." Stiglitz [11] argues that globalization could help to reduce poverty and serve both the developed and developing countries if approached with an appropriate attitude. He also believes that the main requirement for the success of globalization is the "establishment of an equitable playing field."

In the initial stages of globalization, multinational companies purchased their raw materials from any place in the world, wherever is the cheapest; conducted the production of goods and services in any country wherever it is cheapest (where the labour costs were the least), adding their brand and image to the product; and sold their goods and services in any country, in the markets where they can get the best price. Functioning of the mechanism of free trade has effectively increased global trade and global income.

But at the same time, globalization generated the painful consequences of exploitation of natural resources and abuses of labour in countries with lower production costs. The corporations of developed countries moved their production to the countries with abundant cheap labour; labourers of the developed countries started losing their jobs due to relocation in less-developed countries, increasing unemployment. All this leads to environmental degradation and growing inequalities in income distribution. These negative consequences, which were not consistent with the aspirations of people and society, have generated a strong desire for "fair trade" in a global society. Direct results of globalization are such as to encourage the involvement in accordance with the same slogan: "fair trade, not free trade [12]."

1. What is fair trade, and how is it different from free trade?

2. How does free trade impact globalization?

EXCERPT FROM "COMPETING CONCEPTIONS OF GLOBALIZATION," BY LESLIE SKLAIR, FROM THE *JOURNAL OF WORLD-SYSTEMS RESEARCH*, SUMMER 1999

MAIN APPROACHES TO GLOBALIZATION

As with other topics in sociology, there are several ways to categorize theory and research on globalization. One common approach is to compare mono-causal with multi-causal explanations of the phenomenon, as does McGrew (1992). This is a useful way of looking at the problem but it has two main drawbacks. First, it ends up by putting thinkers with entirely different types of explanations—for example those who see globalization as a consequence of the development of material-technological forces and those who see it as a consequence of ideological and/or cultural forces—in the same bag. Second, few thinkers present an entirely mono-causal explanation of anything; most of the thinkers McGrew identifies as mono-causal do try to show the relevance of a variety of factors even if they tend to prioritize some factors over others, while those he identifies as multi-causal do not always argue that everything causes everything else. Globalization, by its very nature, is a big and complex subject.

A second approach is to compare the disciplinary focus of globalization studies. This is certainly an interesting and fruitful avenue to explore: several disciplines have made distinctive contributions to the study of globalization (to some extent all the social sciences have contributed to the debate, but anthropology, geography and international political economy in addition to sociology, can be singled out). These contributions are commonly borrowed by sociologists of globalization, and vice versa, and this will be reflected in my own categorization. I have chosen to categorize globalization studies on the basis of four research clusters in which groups of scholars are working on similar research problems, either in direct contact with each other or, more commonly, in rather indirect contact. Accordingly, I identify the following four sources of globalization research in contemporary sociology:

1. The world-systems approach;

2. The global culture approach;

3. The global society approach;

4. The global capitalism approach.

1. THE WORLD-SYSTEMS APPROACH

This approach is based on the distinction between core, semi peripheral and peripheral countries in terms of their changing roles in the international division of labour dominated by the capitalist world-system. World-systems as a model in social science research, inspired by the work of Immanuel Wallerstein, has been developed in a large and continually expanding body of literature since the 1970s (see Wallerstein 1979, and Shannon, 1989 for a good overview).

The world-systems approach is, unlike the others to be discussed, not only a collection of academic writings but also a highly institutionalized academic enterprise. It is based at the Braudel Center at SUNY Binghamton, supports various international joint academic ventures, and publishes the journal, *Review*. Though the work of world-systems theorists cannot be said to be fully a part of the globalization literature as such (*see* King, ed., 1990), the institutionalization of the world-systems approach undoubtedly prepared the ground for globalization in the social sciences.

In some senses, Wallerstein and his school could rightly claim to have been "global" all along—after all, what could be more global than the "world system"? However, there is no specific concept of the 'global' in most world systems literature. Reference to the "global" comes mainly from critics and, significantly, can be traced to the long-standing problems that the world-system model has had with "cultural issues." Wallerstein's essay on "Culture as the Ideological Battleground of the Modern World-System," the critique by Boyne, and Wallerstein's attempt to rescue his position under the title of "Culture is the World-System" all in Featherstone, ed. 1990), illustrate the problem well.

Chase-Dunn, in his suggestively titled book *Global Formation* (1989), does try to take the argument a stage further by arguing for a dual logic approach to economy and polity. At the economic level, he argues, a global logic of the world-economy prevails whereas at the level of politics a state centred logic of the world-system prevails. However, as the world-economy is basically still explicable only in terms of national economies (countries of the core, semiperiphery and periphery), Chase-Dunn's formulation largely reproduces the problems of Wallerstein's state-centrist analysis.

There is, therefore, no distinctively "global" dimension in the world-systems model apart from the international focus that it has always emphasized. Wallerstein himself rarely uses the word "globalization." For him, the *economics* of the model rests on the international division of labour that distinguishes core, semiperiphery and periphery countries. The *politics* are mostly bound up with antisystemic movements and "superpower struggles." And the *cultural*, insofar as it is dealt with at all, covers debates about the "national" and the "universal" and the concept of "civilization(s)" in the social sciences. Many critics are not convinced that the world-systems model, usually considered to be "economistic" (that is, too locked into economic factors) can deal with cultural issues adequately. Wolff tellingly comments on the way in which the concept of "culture" has been inserted into Wallerstein's world-system model: "An economism which gallantly switches its attentions to the operations of culture is still economism (in King ed., 1991, p.168)." Wallerstein's attempts to theorize "race" nationality and ethnicity in terms of what he refers to as different types of "peoplehood" in the world-system

(Wallerstein, 1991) might be seen as a move in the right direction, but few would argue that cultural factors are an important part of the analysis.

While it would be fair to say that there are various remarks and ideas that do try to take the world-systems model beyond state-centrism[5], any conceptions of the global that world-system theorists have tend to be embedded in the world-economy based on the system of nation-states. The "global" and the "inter-national" are generally used inter-changeably by world-systems theorists. This is certainly one possible use of "global" but it seems quite superfluous, given that the idea of the "inter-national" is so common in the social science literature. Whatever the fate of the world-systems approach, it is unlikely that ideas of globalization would have spread so quickly and deeply in sociology without the impetus it gave to looking at the whole world.

2. GLOBAL CULTURE MODEL

A second model of globalization derives specifically from research on the "globalization of culture." The global culture approach focuses on the problems that a homogenizing mass media-based culture poses for national identities. As we shall see below, this is complementary to, rather than in contradiction with, the global society approach, which focuses more on ideas of an emerging global consciousness and their implications for global community, governance and security.

This is well illustrated in the collection of articles in book-form from the journal *Theory, Culture and Society* (TCS) edited by Featherstone (1990) under the title *Global Culture*. TCS has brought together groups of likeminded theorists through the journal and conferences, which has resulted in an institutional framework and an intellectual critical mass for the development of a culturalist approach to globalization. Of the writers associated with TCS who have made notable contributions to this effort, Robertson—who has been credited with introducing the term globalization into sociology (Waters 1995, p.2)—is probably the most influential.

Although these researchers cannot be identified as a school in the same way as world-system researchers can be, their works do constitute a relatively coherent whole. First, they tend to prioritize the cultural over the political and/or the economic. Second, there is a common interest in the question of how individual and/or national identity can survive in the face of an emerging "global culture."

A distinctive feature of this model is that it problematises the existence of "global culture," as a reality, a possibility or a fantasy. This is based on the very rapid growth that has taken place over the last few decades in the scale of the mass media of communication and the emergence of what Marshall McLuhan famously called "the global village." The basic idea is that the spread of the mass media, especially television, means that everyone in the world can be exposed to the same images, almost instantaneously. This, the argument goes, turns the whole world into a sort of "global village."

Of considerable interest to sociologists theorizing and researching globalization is the distinctive contribution of anthropologists to these debates. Friedman, a Swedish anthropologist, argues, for example, that: "Ethnic and cultural fragmentation and modernist homogenization are not two arguments, two opposing views of what is happening in the world today, but two constitutive trends of global reality. The dualist centralized world of the double East-West hegemony is fragmenting, politically, and culturally, but the homogeneity of capitalism remains as intact and as systematic as ever" (in Featherstone 1990:311). While not all would agree either that capitalism remains intact and systematic or that it is, in fact, the framework of globalization, the fragmentation of "the double East-West hegemony" is beyond doubt. Ideas such as hybridization and creolization have been proposed in the effort to try to conceptualize what happens when people and items from different (sometimes, but not always, dominant and subordinate) cultures interact.[6]

Some globalization of culture' theorists have also contributed to current debates on postmodernity in which transformations in the mass media and media representations of reality and so-called "hyperreality" play a central role. Indicative of similar interests is a compilation of articles edited by Albrow and King (1990) which raised several central issues relevant to the ideas of global sociology, global society and globalization, as new problem areas in the social sciences. One important emphasis has been the "globalization" of sociology itself as a discipline. This connects in some important ways with the debate about the integrity of national cultures in a globalizing world. While the classical sociological theorists, notably Marx, Weber and Durkheim, all tried to generalize about how societies changed and tried to establish some universal features of social organization, none of them saw the need to theorize on the global level. This connects in some important ways with the debate about the integrity of national cultures in a globalizing world, and particularly the influence of "Western" economic, political, military and cultural forms on non-Western societies.

GLOBO-LOCALISM

A subset of the global culture approach, characterised as "globo-localism," derives from a group of scholars from various countries and social science traditions whose main concern is to try to make sense of the multifaceted and enormously complex web of local-global relations. There is a good deal of overlap between this and the "globalization of culture" model, but the globo-local researchers tend to emphasize the "territorial" dimension.

This view has been actively developed within the International Sociological Association (ISA). The ISA 12th World Congress of Sociology in Madrid in the 1990 was organized around the theme "Sociology for One World: Unity and Diversity." Mlinar (ed., 1992) reports that 'the issue of globalization was readily accepted' and his edited volume of papers from the conference illustrates the variety of issues raised in Madrid. The 1994 ISA Congress in Bielefeld, Germany, continued the theme under the title: "Contested Boundaries and Shifting Solidarities" and again discussions of globalization were quite prominently featured on the agenda, and the 1998 Conference in Montreal continues the trend. It is not surprising that globalization and territory attracted attention, for in the background to the 1990 and 1994 conferences the wars in the former Yugoslavia were raging (Mlinar himself is from Slovenia, formerly part of Yugoslavia) and, of course, the first shocks of the end of the communist state system were giving way to new territorial issues created by an explosive mix of local and global forces.

If Mlinar is a European progenitor of the globo-local model, then the American progenitor is Alger (1988) who developed the concept of the "local-global nexus." There is no single common theoretical position in the work of Mlinar, Alger and the others involved in this enterprise. What unites them is the urge to theorize and research questions of what happens to *territorial identities* (within and across countries) in a globalizing world. Thus, it is part of the more general global culture model, but with a distinct territorial focus.

The main research question for all these writers is the autonomy of local cultures in the face of an advancing "global culture." Competing claims of local cultures against the forces of 'globalization' have forced themselves onto the sociological, cultural and political agendas all over the world. This is largely continuous with the focus of the third globalization model, based on the idea of global society.

3. GLOBAL SOCIETY MODELS

Inspiration for this general conception of globalization is often located in the pictures of planet earth sent back by space explorers. A classic statement of this was the report of Apollo XIV astronaut Edgar Mitchell in 1971:

> It was a beautiful, harmonious, peaceful-looking planet, blue with white clouds, and one that gave you a deep sense ... of home, of being, of identity. It is what I prefer to call instant global consciousness.[7]

Had astronaut Mitchell penetrated a little through the clouds, he would also have seen horrific wars in Vietnam and other parts of Asia, bloody repression by various dictatorial regimes in Africa and Latin America, dead and maimed bodies as a result of sectarian terrorism in Britain and Ireland, as well as a terrible toll of human misery from hunger, disease, drug abuse and carnage on roads all round the world as automobile cultures intensified their own peculiar structures of globalization. Nevertheless, some leading globalization theorists, for example Giddens (1991) and Robertson (1992), do attribute great significance to ideas like global awareness' and 'planetary consciousness'.

Historically, global society theorists argue that the concept of world or global society has become a believable idea only in the modern age and, in particular, science, technology, industry and universal values are increasingly creating a twentieth century world that is different from any past age. The globalization literature is full of discussions of the decreasing power and significance of the nation-state and the increasing significance (if not actually power) of supra-national and global institutions and systems of belief. Ideas of space-time distanciation (see Giddens, 1991) and of time-space compression (see Harvey, 1989) illustrate how processes of globalization compress, stretch and deepen space-time for people all over the world thus creating some of the conditions for a global society.

In his attempt to order the field of globalization studies, Spybey (1996) contrasts the view that "modernity is inherently globalizing" (Giddens, 1991, p.63) with the view that globalization predates modernity (Robertson, 1992). While Spybey comes down in favour of Giddens thesis that globalization is best conceptualized as "reflexive modernization," he is less clear about why these differences matter and, in the end, as with so many debates in the social sciences, the main protagonists seem to be saying more or less the same things in rather different languages. However, it is important to establish whether globalization is a new name for a relatively old phenomenon (which appears to be the argument of Robertson), or whether it is relatively new, a phenomenon of late modernity (the argument of Giddens) or whether it is very new and primarily a consequence of post-1960s capitalism (the argument of Sklair). Why does this matter? It matters because if we want to understand our own lives and the lives of those around us, in our families, communities, local regions, countries, supra-national regions and, ultimately how we relate to the global, then it is absolutely fundamental that we are clear about the extent to which the many different structures within which we live are the same in the most important respects as they have been or are different. Two critics, in their attempt to demonstrate that globalization is a myth because the global economy does not really exist, argue that there is 'no fundamental difference between the international submarine telegraph cable method of financial transactions [of the early twentieth century] and contemporary electronic systems (Hirst and Thompson, 1996, p.197). They are entirely mistaken. The fundamental difference is, precisely, in the way that the electronics revolution (a post-1960s phenomenon) has transformed the quantitative possibilities of transferring cash and money capital into qualitatively new forms of corporate and personal financing, entrepreneurship and, crucially, the system of credit on which the global culture and ideology of consumerism largely rests. Some globalization theorists argue forcefully that these phenomena are all new and fundamental for understanding not only what is happening in the rich countries, but in social groups anywhere who have a part to play in this global system. In this sense the idea of a global society is a very provocative one but, while it is relatively easy to establish empirically the objective dimensions of globalization as they involve the large majority of the world's population, the idea of a global society based on subjective relationships to globalization, planetary consciousness and the like, is highly speculative.[8]

There appears to be, however, a real psychological need for many writers to believe in the possibilities of a global society (which I share).[9] As McGrew (1992) shows, this theme is elaborated by scholars grappling with the apparent contradictions between globalization and local disruption and strife based on ethnic and other particularistic loyalties. It is in this type of approach that a growing appreciation of the ethical problems of globalization is particularly to be found. The reason for this is simple: now that humankind has the capacity to destroy itself through war and toxic accidents of various types, a democratic and just human society on the global level, however utopian, seems to be the best long-term guarantee of the continued survival of humanity (Held 1995).

4. GLOBAL CAPITALISM MODEL

A fourth model of globalization locates the dominant global forces in the structures of an ever-more globalizing capitalism (for example, Ross and Trachte 1990, Sklair 1995, McMichael 1996; see also Robinson 1996). While all of these writers and others who could be identified with this approach develop their own specific analyses of globalization, they all strive towards a concept of the "global" that involves more than the relations between nation-states and state-centrist explanations of national economies competing against each other.

Ross and Trachte focus specifically on capitalism as a social system which is best analyzed on three levels, namely the level of the internal logic of the system (inspired by Marx and Adam Smith), the structural level of historical development and the level of the specific social formation, or society. They explain the deindustrialization of some of the heartland regions of capitalism and the transformations of what we still call the Third World in these terms and argue that the globalization of the capitalist system is deeply connected to the capitalist crises of the 1970s and after (oil price shocks, rising unemployment, and increasing insecurity as the rich countries experience problems in paying for their welfare states). This leads them to conclude that: "We are only at the beginning of the global era" (Ross and Trachte, 1990, p.230).

Sklair proposes a more explicit model of the global system based on the concept of *transnational practices*, practices that originate with non-state actors and cross state borders. They are analytically distinguished in three spheres: economic, political and cultural-ideological. Each of these practices is primarily, but not exclusively, characterized by a major institution. The *transnational corporation* (TNC) is the most important institution for economic transnational practices; the *transnational capitalist class* (TCC) for political transnational practices; and the *culture-ideology of consumerism* for transnational cultural-ideological practices (Sklair 1995). The research agenda of this theory is concerned with how TNCs, transnational capitalist classes and the culture-ideology of consumerism operate to transform the world in terms of the global capitalist project. [...]

The culture-ideology of consumerism prioritizes the exceptional place of consumption and consumerism in contemporary capitalism, increasing consumption expectations and aspirations without necessarily ensuring the income to buy. The extent to which economic and environmental constraints on the private accumulation of capital challenge the global capitalist project in general and its culture-ideology of consumerism in particular, is a central issue for global system theory (Sklair in Redclift and Benton 1994; see also Durning 1992).

McMichael (1996) focuses on the issue of Third World development and provides both theoretical and empirical support for the thesis that globalization is a qualitatively new phenomenon and not simply a quantitative expansion of older trends. He contrasts two periods. First, the "Development Project" (late 1940s to early 1970s), when all countries tried to develop their national economies with the help of international development agencies and institutions. The second period he labels the "Globalization Project" (1980s onwards), when development is pursued through attempts to integrate economies into a globalized world market, and the process is directed by a public-private coalition of "Global Managers." He explains:

> As parts of national economies became embedded more deeply in global enterprise through commodity chains, they weakened as national units and strengthened the reach of the global economy. This situation was not unique to the 1980s, but the mechanisms of the debt regime institutionalized the power and authority of global management within states' very organization and procedures. This was the turning point in the story of development. (McMichael 1996, p.135)

This contribution to the debate is notable for its many telling empirical examples of the effects of globalization on Third World communities.

To these writers on globalization and capitalism we can add other Marxist and Marx-inspired scholars who see capitalism as a global system, but do not have any specific concepts of globalization. The most important of these is the geographer, David Harvey, whose Marxist analysis of modernity and postmodernity is significant for the attempt to build a bridge between the debates around economic and cultural globalization (Harvey, 1989, especially chapter 15).

SUMMING-UP THE APPROACHES

Each of the four approaches to globalization has its own distinctive strengths and weaknesses. The world-system model tends to be economistic (minimizing the importance of political and cultural factors), but as globalization is often interpreted in terms of economic actors and economic institutions, this does seem to be a realistic approach. The globalization of culture model, on the other hand, tends to be culturalist (minimizing economic factors), but as much of the criticism of globalization comes from those who focus on the negative effects of homogenizing mass media and marketing on local and indigenous cultures, the culturalist approach has many adherents. The world society model tends to be both optimistic and all-inclusive, an excellent combination for the production of world-views, but less satisfactory for social science research programmes. Finally, the global capitalism model, by prioritising the global capitalist system and paying less attention to other global forces, runs the risk of appearing one-sided. However, the question remains: how important is that "one side" (global capitalism).[10]

RESISTANCES TO GLOBALIZATION

Globalization is often seen in terms of impersonal forces wreaking havoc on the lives of ordinary and defence-less people and communities. It is not coincidental that interest in globalization over the last two decades has been accompanied by an upsurge in what has come to be known as New Social Movements (NSM) research (Ray 1993, Spybey 1996, chapter 7, Sklair 1998b). NSM theorists, despite their substantial differences, argue that the traditional response of the labour movement to global capitalism, based on class politics, has generally failed, and that a new analysis based on identity politics (of gender, sexuality, ethnicity, age, community, belief systems) is necessary to mount effective resistance to sexism, racism, environmental damage, warmongering, capitalist exploitation and other forms of injustice.

The globalization of identity politics involves the establishment of global networks of people with similar identities and interests outside the control of international, state and local authorities. There is a substantial volume of research and documentation on such developments in the women's, peace and environmental movements, some of it in direct response to governmental initiatives (for example, alternative and NGO organization shadowing official United Nations and other conferences) but most theorists and activists tend to operate under the slogan: think global, act local (Ekins, 1992).

The main challenges to global capitalism in the economic sphere have also come from those who "think global and act local." This normally involves disrupting the capacity of TNCs and global financial institutions to accumulate private profits at the expense of their workforces, their consumers and the communities which are affected by their activities. An important part of economic globalization today is the increasing dispersal of the manufacturing process into many discrete phases carried out in many different places. Being no longer so dependent on the production of one factory and one workforce gives capital a distinct advantage, particularly against the strike weapon which once gave tremendous negative power to the working class. Global production chains can be disrupted by strategically planned stoppages, but these generally act more as inconveniences than as real weapons of labour against capital. The international division of labour and its corollary, the globalization of production, builds flexibility into the system so that not only can capital migrate anywhere in the world to find the cheapest reliable productive sources of labour but also few workforces can any longer decisively "hold capital to ransom" by withdrawing their labour. At the level of the production process, globalizing capital has all but defeated labour. In this respect, the global organization of the TNCs and allied institutions like globalizing government agencies and the World Bank have, so far, proved too powerful for the local organization of labour and communities.

Nevertheless, the global capitalists, if we are to believe their own propaganda, are continuously beset by opposition, boycott, legal challenge and moral outrage from the consumers of their products and by disruptions from their workers. There are also many ways to be ambivalent or hostile about global capitalism and cultures and ideologies of consumerism, some of which have been successfully exploited by the "Green" movement (see Mander and Goldsmith, eds. 1996).

The issue of democracy is central to the advance of the forces of globalization and the practices and the prospects of social movements that oppose them, both local and global. The rule of law, freedom of association and expression, freely contested elections, as minimum conditions and however imperfectly sustained, are as necessary in the long run for mass market based global consumerist capitalism as they are for alternative social systems.

CONCLUSION

This account of the state of globalization studies to date has focused on what distinguishes global from inter-national forces, processes and institutions. It is almost exclusively based on the European and North American literature and it does not preclude the possibility of other and quite different conceptions of globalization being developed elsewhere. Despite the view, particularly evident in the accounts of "global culture" theorists that globalization is more or less the same as Westernization or Americanization or McDonaldization (Ritzer, 1995), more and more critics are beginning to question this one-way traffic bias in the globalization literature. This critique is well-represented in the empirical cases and analytical points of those who are "Interrogating Theories of the Global" (in King ed., 1991, chapter 6) and the work of African and Asian scholars represented in Albrow and King (eds. 1990), all of whom provide some necessary correctives to European-North American orthodoxies. These scholars, and others, are doing important research relevant for the study of globalization, and their work does not necessarily fit into the four approaches identified above. It is very likely that an introduction to globalization studies to be written ten years from now will reflect non-Western perspectives much more strongly. Nevertheless, although of quite recent vintage, it is undeniable that globalization as a theoretical issue and an object of research, is now firmly on the agenda of the social sciences.

1. Should economists take into account the cultural impact of globalization when creating trade deals? Why or why not?

2. Choose one of the approaches described by the author. Do you agree with it? Why or why not?

EXCERPT FROM "GLOBALIZATION AND WORKERS IN DEVELOPING COUNTRIES," BY MARTIN RAMA, FROM THE WORLD BANK DEVELOPMENT RESEARCH GROUP, JANUARY 2003

4. JOB DESTRUCTION AND JOB CREATION

Looking at the average wage, or even at the wage distribution, is not enough to understand how globalization can affect individual workers. Specific groups could experience large gains or losses due to globalization. But if these groups are small, or if their movements up and down the ladder cancel each other, the impact on the average wage or the wage distribution may not be visible. The more substantial the churning effects, the more likely that globalization will be resisted by the potential losers. Job creation and job destruction are important mechanisms through which churning may occur. But the very nature of some continuing jobs can also change in the process. This is what happens when a worker ceases to be covered by a collective bargaining agreement, or when a permanent worker who enjoys all the perks and benefits extended by formal labor regulations is replaced by a temporary worker with limited rights.

A series of case studies on the effects of trade liberalization shows a considerable dispersion of the net impact on employment. In some countries, net job losses were quite minimal. In Morocco, for example, employment in the average private sector manufacturing firm was basically unaffected by trade liberalization (Currie and Harrison, 1997). The shift in labor demand was modest in Mexico as well (Revenga, 1997). But in Uruguay, in a period in which trade union activities were banned, the decline was substantial. During that period, reducing the protection rate within a sector by one percent led of an employment reduction between 0.4 and 0.5 percent within the same year. The employment effect became much smaller when trade union activities were allowed (Ramna, 1994).

Small declines in employment may hide substantial job churning however. The contrast between studies at the industry level and at the firm level is revealing in this respect. Seddon and Wacziarg (2001) used industry-level data to examine the impact of trade liberalization episodes on movements of labor across sectors. Their study found some labor reallocation between narrowly defined manufacturing activities. But the estimated effects were statistically insignificant and small in magnitude. On the other hand, Levinsohn (1999) used firm-level data to examine the pattern of job creation and job destruction in Chile during trade liberalization. Whereas net employment in manufacturing fell by about 8 percent, in all years in this period about a quarter of all workers changed jobs.

Globalization also affected the nature of jobs in formerly protected sectors. In Morocco, there were significant employment losses in specific groups of firms, which started to rely more on low-pay, temporary workers. The share of temporary employment in manufacturing rose by nearly twenty percentage points between 1984 and 1990. In Mexico, trade reform reduced the rents available to be captured by firms and workers. As a result, an average tariff reduction of 20 percentage points led to an implied wage reduction of more than 5 percent. In Uruguay, trade liberalization was associated with lower wages in the period when trade unions were not active, despite the considerable reduction in employment. In the period with active unions, the membership rate was strongly correlated with tariff barriers and concentration at the industry level. This correlation suggests that workers in protected sectors enjoy higher wages and better working conditions than their counterparts in sectors exposed to foreign competition.

Overall, these studies show that there was pervasive rent sharing between the protected enterprises and their workers. The removal of trade barriers makes workers lose those rents, either because they lose their jobs altogether, or because the rent attached to their jobs becomes smaller. This interpretation is consistent with the one offered for the effect of globalization on the gender gap in earnings. In both cases, increased competition in product markets appears to reduce the size of labor market rents enjoyed by either employers or employees. On the other hand, there is no strong evidence to support the claim that labor demand has become more elastic as a result of globalization (Chinoy, Krisna, and Mitra, 1998; Maloney and Fajnzylber, 2000).

Another source of job destruction has been the downsizing of state-owned enterprises and government agencies. The most dramatic retrenchment episodes took place in transition economies, where millions of workers needed to be reallocated to the private sector. But all regions in the world have had their dose of downsizing in recent years (Haltiwanger and Singh, 1999; Kikeri, 1997). In some cases, up to a half of the workforce in state-owned enterprises needs to be considered redundant, if those enterprises are to be run as private firms (Belser and Rama, 2001). It could be argued that public sector downsizing is not directly connected to globalization, but the two are not independent either. Countries that remain isolated from the outside world can keep their state sectors untouched for much longer.

Studies following public sector workers after retrenchment, or comparing their earnings and benefits to those of similar private sector workers, reveal a consistent pattern of losses from job separation (Rama, 1999). Other things equal, the decline in earnings and benefits is smaller for more educated workers, and larger for those with more seniority in the public sector. However, the total loss may not be as large for the latter, as they usually have fewer years of work before retirement. Studies focused on welfare, rather than just earnings and benefits, also show larger losses for workers with more dependents. Finally, women can also lose more than men. They are not necessarily more likely to be targeted by downsizing programs, but they are more likely to experience a large drop in earnings. The gender gap in earnings tends to be smaller in the public sector than out of it, implying a bigger loss, in relative terms, for separated women. Moreover, the public sector usually offers benefits that are highly valued by women, such as maternity leave, flexibility of hours and daycare facilities. These benefits are more rare in the private sector, and generally unavailable in the informal sector, where most of the new jobs taken by separated workers are. Not surprisingly, women are more likely than men to withdraw from the labor force after downsizing (Rama and MacIsaac, 1999).

Globalization has also led to substantial job creation, however. The most visible part of this creation is associated with foreign direct investment and, particularly, with export-processing zones. The latter are often defined as fenced-in industrial estates specializing in manufacturing for exports that offer free-trade conditions and a liberal regulatory environment. But this definition is too restrictive. In countries like China or Mauritius, firms are not geographically constrained in industrial estates. In others, they are allowed to sell part of their output in the domestic market (Madani, 1999). In theory, export-processing zones represent a sub-optimal mechanism to integrate a country with world markets, the optimum being to offer free-trade conditions and a liberal regulatory environment across the board. In some countries, such as Sri Lanka, social and political constraints may prevent the complete removal of barriers and regulations in sectors with powerful vested interests. In this case, export-processing zones can be seen as a way to reform "at the margin". In other countries, like China, special zones have been a way to experiment market-oriented reforms.

Regardless of their theoretical merits, export-processing zones have been a powerful engine of employment generation. [...] The case of Mauritius is outstanding. But the share is considerable in several of the other countries as well, especially when taking into account that agricultural activities and the informal sector still employ a considerable fraction of the labor force.

On the other hand, jobs in the export-processing zones are not as good as the "privileged" jobs in protected activities or in the public sector. One of the features of these zones is their flexibility with labor laws. In some countries, the flexibility is explicit. For instance, prior to 1993 the Dominican Republic law did not impose the minimum wage on export-processing zones. In other countries, the zones are not excluded from labor laws, but the latter are not enforced either. Lax governmental supervision and opposition to labor unionization and union activities are common. As a result, jobs in export-processing zones are less secure than formal sector jobs out of them. As regards wages and working conditions, they vary substantially depending on the size, nationality and corporate policy of the firm, the type of industrial production, labor market conditions and the country's institutions and regulations.

Most of the jobs in export-processing zones are held by women. In the Caribbean zones approximately 80 percent of the workforce is female, and the percentage is almost as high in the Philippines. This female bias is especially strong in garment production. Several reasons have been advanced to explain why women, many young and single, are sought after as prospective employees. Women are said to be more diligent and have more dexterity than men. Also, the fact that most of them marry and leave after a few years implies that they tend not to get involved with trade unions. Last but not least, women tend to be paid less than men. Madani concludes that, despite their lower pay, women might be the unintended beneficiaries from the formation of export-processing zones. Many would have remained fully or partially employed in the informal sector, or stayed at home, were it not for them.

The pattern is similar in countries that have not relied massively on export-processing zones, but where exporting firms have tapped local labor markets, attracting workers from the surrounding villages. Industries such as textiles and electronics have massively hired young, literate, largely single women, who frequently ended up earning more than in traditional sectors, such as agriculture or cottage industries. This female bias has been observed even out of the wage sector. Evidence from Ghana and Uganda reveals that women had substantial economic mobility in response to economic reforms. In these two countries, rural women became increasingly engaged in non-farm employment activities, moving into the non-farm sector at faster rates than men (World Bank, 2001).

To the extent that globalization does translate into significant job creation in developing countries, the potential impact on poverty can be dramatic. But this impact depends significantly on where the job creation occurs. In China much of the impetus for the rapid economic growth during the 1980s came from a tremendous expansion of rural township and village enterprise activities. These firms often emerged out of the community level structures which had been in place prior to the introduction of the house-hold responsibility system in agriculture in the late 1970s, and typically became involved in labor-intensive export oriented manufacturing activities (Byrd and Lin, eds., 1990). The inroads into rural poverty which were achieved in China during this period were nothing short of remarkable (World Bank, 2000b). In other parts of the developing world a simi-larly strong negative relationship between poverty and the non-farm sector has been observed. Even where non-farm employment opportunities accrue primarily to the relatively educated and skilled (and thus non-poor), benefits to the poor are often still discernable. This is due to the relationship between the wage rates earned by agricultural laborers in rural areas, who are generally highly represented among the poor, and the tightening of rural labor markets which gener-ally accompanies an expanding non-farm sector (Lanjouw and Lanjouw, 2000).

On the other hand, there is a legitimate concern that participation in world markets may be associated with an increase in child labor. The latter could have a detrimental effect on child welfare, both in the short term and in the longer term, though reduced schooling. Policy reforms that promote labor-intensive production could therefore be a mixed blessing for the poor. For example, a recent study of child labor in a city in western India concluded that: "The prevalence and absolute expansion of child labor in a period and region of relatively high growth of aggre-gate output indicates that the nature of economic growth is flawed" (Swaminathan, 1998, page 1526). The argu-ment merits closer scrutiny. An important issue is whether sectors exposed to international competition tend to be more intensive in child labor. Unfortunately, the evidence in this respect is scattered.

According to statistics assembled by the International Labour Office, about 70 percent of the children who work are employed as unpaid family helpers in rural areas (Ashagrie, 1997). Around 5 percent of all child workers could actually be employed in export industries. A well-known example is the carpet industry in Uttar Pradesh. An International Labour Office survey of carpet-weaving enterprises found that a quarter of the workers were less than 14 years old. Children and adults perform the same job in these enterprises, with roughly the same productivity. But children workers have lower wages. Given how competitive the industry is, some argue that small loom owners would not be able to absorb the decrease in profits, were child labor banned. Garment manufacturing in Bangladesh was another notorious example. However, enterprises stopped employing children under 14 years of age due to a consumer boycott in industrial countries. It is through the sex industry that globalization could have its most adverse impact on the children of developing countries. Lower travel costs and better information networks may be associated with a growth in sexual tourism, including pedophilia. The children affected may only represent a tiny fraction of all the children who work. But the implications for their well-being are dramatic enough to warrant swift public action.

1. What are some of the economic benefits of free trade?

2. What are some of the issues created by free trade?

CHAPTER 2

WHAT THE GOVERNMENT AND POLITICIANS SAY

Trade deals are made by the president and ratified by Congress, making them important legislative decisions that are shaped by presidential initiatives. Free trade deals have been popular with both Republicans and Democrats since the 1930s, when President Franklin D. Roosevelt began introducing them as a way to help reduce agricultural surpluses. For decades, free trade was seen as a beneficial system by which American-made goods could be traded around the world for low costs to manufacturers. But in recent years the debate has become more heated as some politicians feel more needs to be done to protect US manufacturers as low-cost goods from around

the world flood the United States market and
drive down costs. Others believe free trade deals,
which can help economic growth, should not be
given to countries with which we do not agree
on fundamental issues, including human rights.
There remains much disccord about not only the
efficacy and consequences of free trade, but with
which partners countries should enter into free
trade agreements. Oftentimes, the loudest voices
in these debates over free trade and globalization are politicians—some of whose opinions are
represented in this chapter.

"JOINT LETTER IN FAVOR OF TRADE PROMOTION AUTHORITY," ALAN GREENSPAN AND FORMER CHAIRS OF THE PRESIDENT'S COUNCIL OF ECONOMIC ADVISERS, FROM THE US HOUSE OF REPRESENTATIVES COMMITTEE ON WAYS AND MEANS, MARCH 5, 2015

Dear Mr. Speaker, Mr. Leader, Madam Pelosi, and Senator Reid:

International trade is fundamentally good for the U.S. economy, beneficial to American families over time, and consonant with our domestic priorities. That is why we support the renewal of Trade Promotion Authority (TPA) to make it possible for the United States to reach international agreements with our economic partners in Asia through the Trans-Pacific Partnership (TPP) and in Europe through the Transatlantic Trade and Investment Partnership (TTIP). Trade Promotion Authority provides for an up or down vote on these agreements, without amendments, and thereby encourages our trade partners to put their best offers on the table.

Expanded trade through these agreements will contribute to higher incomes and stronger productivity growth over time in both the United States and other countries. U.S. businesses will enjoy improved access to overseas markets, while the greater variety of choices and lower prices trade brings will allow household budgets to go further to the benefit of American families.

Trade is beneficial for our society as a whole, but the benefits are unevenly distributed and some people are negatively affected by increased global competition. The economy-wide benefits resulting from increased trade provide resources to make progress on important social goals, including helping those who are adversely affected.

Increased global economic engagement will enhance U.S. global leadership in line with our values. Indeed, trade agreements signed under both Democratic and Republican Presidents have included provisions to combat corruption and to strengthen environment and labor standards.

It is not desirable for trade agreements to include provisions aimed at so-called currency manipulation. This is because monetary policy affects the value of currencies. Attempts to penalize countries for supposedly manipulating exchange rates would thus impose constraints on U.S. monetary policy, to the detriment of all Americans.

We believe that agreements to foster greater international trade are in our national economic and security interests, and support a renewal of Trade Promotion Authority.

Alan Greenspan, Greenspan Associates (1974 to 1977)
Charles L. Schultze, Brookings Institution (1977 to 1981)
Martin Feldstein, Harvard University (1982 to 1984)
Michael J. Boskin, Stanford University (1989 to 1993)
Laura D'Andrea Tyson, UC Berkeley (1993 to 1995)
Martin N. Baily, Brookings Institution (1999 to 2001)
R. Glenn Hubbard, Columbia University (2001 to 2003)

N. Gregory Mankiw, Harvard University (2003 to 2005)
Harvey S. Rosen, Princeton University (2005)
Ben S. Bernanke, Brookings Institution (2005 to 2006)
Edward P. Lazear, Stanford University (2006 to 2009)
Christina D. Romer, UC Berkeley (2009 to 2010)
Austan D. Goolsbee, University of Chicago (2010 to 2011)
Alan B. Krueger, Princeton University, (2011 to 2013)

The letter writers were chairs of the President's Council of Economic Advisers under Presidents Gerald Ford, Jimmy Carter, Ronald Reagan, George H.W. Bush, William J. Clinton, George W. Bush, and Barack Obama.

1. Why do these economists support free trade agreements?

"CONGRESSIONAL RECORD: H.R. 3087 COLOMBIA FREE TRADE AGREEMENT, H.R. 3079 PANAMA FREE TRADE AGREEMENT, H.R. 3080 SOUTH KOREA FREE TRADE AGREEMENT, H.R. 2832 TAA AND GSP EXTENSION," BY THE HONORARY BETTY MCCOLLUM, REPRESENTATIVE OF MINNESOTA, FROM THE US HOUSE OF REPRESENTATIVES, OCTOBER 12, 2011

Mr. Speaker, I rise today in opposition to the three trade agreements this House is considering with Colombia, Panama, and South Korea, respectively. At a time when our national unemployment rate is at 9.1 percent, with 14 million Americans looking for work, we cannot afford to pass trade agreements that cost jobs here in the United States. Instead, I urge my colleagues to bring a real jobs bill—one that will create jobs for American workers—to the floor of the House immediately.

America depends on trade with countries around the world to expand export markets for our products and create good-paying jobs in the U.S. To achieve fair trade, agreements must not export U.S. jobs or economically harm communities. We must insist that all trade agreements promote environmental sustainability, workers' rights, and improved living standards for people throughout the world. The negotiated trade agreements with Colombia, Panama, and South Korea do not meet the standard of fair trade agreements and will leave Americans worse off. I do not support their passage.

In Colombia, the intimidation and murder of trade unionists and human rights workers is widespread. According to Human Rights Watch, over 50 trade unionists were murdered last year. The Colombian government's human rights record may be improving but it is still very poor. This is not the time to reward Colombia's poor record with a preferential trade arrangement. This agreement does not advance fair trade, and I urge my colleagues to vote against it.

The proposed free trade agreement with Panama fails to create any American jobs. Widely known as a tax haven for multinational corporations, Panama has not shown the inclination or ability to change its status as an off-shore tax shelter. This practice rewards U.S. companies that ship jobs overseas to avoid taxation here. This agreement does not advance fair trade, and I urge my colleagues to vote against it.

In South Korea, between 2001 and 2009, the U.S. ran a trade deficit in goods of approximately $125 billion. The Economic Policy Institute found that implementation of the Korea trade deal would increase U.S. trade deficit by $16.7 billion and result in 159,000 American jobs lost over the next seven years. According to Public Citizen, almost 8,000 good-paying jobs would be lost in the 4th Congressional District of Minnesota. This agreement does not advance fair trade, and I urge my colleagues to vote against it.

As we've seen with free trade agreements with China, NAFTA, and CAFTA, unfair trade deals cost American jobs. This is why Trade Adjustment Assistance, TAA, exists—to provide training to workers who lose their jobs due to trade. Considering TAA while we consider these three agreements is evidence that these deals result in the loss of jobs here in the U.S. I support the passage of the needed TM extension, H.R. 2832, in order to provide some protections for American workers.

For these reasons, I urge my colleagues to oppose these unfair trade deals and support the badly-needed extensions of TAA.

1. Why does Representative McCollum oppose these trade agreements?

2. Should the issues she raises be considered when making trade deals? Why or why not?

"FREE PEOPLE AND FREE MARKETS: A VISION FOR THE FUTURE OF THE AMERICAS," BY HOUSE SPEAKER JOHN BOEHNER, COUNCIL FOR THE AMERICAS, FROM SPEAKER PAUL RYAN'S PRESS OFFICE, MAY 8, 2012

It is an honor to address the Council of the Americas, and truly a humbling thing to receive this award.

As the Council notes, its members 'share a common commitment to economic and social development, open markets, the rule of law, and democracy throughout the Western Hemisphere.

These are the principles that have shaped the course of many nations in our region, including the United States. And they are the principles upon which the future of the Americas must rest.

I stand before you today as an admirer of Latin America and a believer in the potential of our hemisphere.

I'm a believer in the power of free markets and free people, and a student of how both, together, have transformed the nations of the Americas and positioned us for the future.

The free enterprise system gave my family the opportunity to succeed, and it has done the same for generations of families throughout our hemisphere, when it has been allowed to flourish.

I was, and am, a strong supporter of NAFTA, CAFTA, and our trade agreements with Peru and Chile, which have led to greater prosperity and security throughout our region. I was, and am, a strong supporter of Plan Colombia and the Merida Initiative, which have been instrumental in securing those gains.

I have had the honor of serving as Speaker of the U.S. House of Representatives now for about a year and a half.

When my colleagues and I took over the House, we did so with a lengthy agenda focused on jobs and the economy.

Most of our agenda has now been passed by the House—and in spite of the challenges of divided government, some of it has been enacted into law.

I'm pleased to say this includes the free trade agreements with Colombia and Panama that were stalled for years under the previous House majority.

Shortly after I was elected by my colleagues to serve as Speaker-designate for the 112th Congress, in fact, President Obama and I had a conversation about trade.

At the time, the United States had free trade agreements pending with three different nations— South Korea, Colombia, and Panama.

The president and I agreed that enacting these agreements would support job creation in the United States.

The president mentioned the idea of moving ahead on one of them—probably Korea—and depending on how that went, maybe talking about moving one of the others.

I told the president that we needed to move on all of them at once. I told him he could be confident that the House would move them swiftly. I urged him to send them all to the Hill at the same time.

And eventually, to his credit, he did. In October 2011, the House and Senate overwhelmingly passed all three trade agreements. And just last month, the president stood with President Santos in Cartagena to announce that the Colombia FTA will formally take effect in May.

In January, just three months after passage of the agreements, I led a bipartisan delegation to Latin America focused on our economic and security partnerships in the region.

One of the highlights of the trip was presenting President Santos, and our Ambassador to Colombia, Michael McKinley, with framed 'red-line' copies of the signed Colombia Free Trade agreement.

The emotion I saw from both men when they were presented with this symbolic gift was genuine.

It spoke volumes about the importance of the agreement for the people of both countries, and the hard work that went into enacting it on both sides.

The impression was reinforced a day later, when, upon learning of our delegation's visit to Colombia, President Martinelli of Panama made an unscheduled trip from Panama City to join us as guests of President Santos.

President Martinelli knew we were going to be talking about implementation of the free trade agreements, and he wanted to be there.

President Martinelli made that impromptu journey across the South Caribbean Sea for the same reason I made my own trip to Latin America: because the friendship and economic partnership among our countries is vital to the future of our region.

When the Colombia Free Trade Agreement enters into force this month, it will be an important moment for the prosperity of our hemisphere.

It is equally important that the Panama Free Trade Agreement be fully implemented in the months ahead.

These trade agreements are a tangible manifestation of how the United States views the region.

They are a roadmap to an enduring partnership among allies, working together as respected and trusted partners.

And it's important that we keep the momentum going.

I'm disappointed the Administration has not moved to build on these achievements by seeking Trade Promotion Authority.

TPA would help to ensure continued expansion of free trade and open markets, to support job creation here at home and abroad.

Trade, though, is but one vital component of our partnership.

Without a sustained political commitment to a common vision based on respect, dignity, and opportunity, the main narrative will continue to be the contest for leadership in Latin America and how the U.S. interacts with the competing blocs.

During my journey to Latin America, I saw vibrant nations brimming with the promise of prosperity, security and democracy.

The nations of the Americas share a hemisphere, but we also share more than that.

We share a respect for democracy, and an appreciation for the superiority of a free economy.

We also share an opportunity—a chance to secure freedom, prosperity and security for our people by working together.

Free-market capitalism and representative democracy go hand in hand, and they have worked hand in hand to lift nations out of chaos and into competitiveness.

I returned from Latin America convinced that our objective should be to make the entire Western Hemisphere a free enterprise zone—free markets, free trade, and free people.

I had a vision of neighbor countries, each with a distinct identity and unique national character, but with a shared, ironclad commitment to freedom and democracy.

It's an attainable vision, but challenges exist. I believe there are three major threats.

The first such threat is Iran, which has made little attempt to disguise its global ambitions, or its interest in gaining a foothold in Latin America that can serve as a base of support for those ambitions.

The same week our delegation was visiting Brazil, Colombia, and Mexico, another foreign leader was conducting a Latin America mission as well.

That leader was Mahmoud Ahmadinejad.

It was telling that his itinerary included none of the nations we visited, including Brazil—which, to President Rousseff's great credit, has spurned Iran's recent advances.

Instead Brazil has opted to pursue a path that demonstrates it seeks a responsible leadership role on the global stage—a role that corresponds with its considerable economic potential and role in the region.

Indeed, while I and the members of our delegation were visiting three of Latin America's most vibrant democracies, Ahmadinejad was being hosted by nations such as Venezuela and Cuba, whose governments have been linked to state-sponsored terrorism and have isolated themselves internationally.

His trip underscored the designs Iran has for expanding its influence in Latin America, and its eagerness to forge bonds with governments in the Western Hemisphere that have demonstrated a lesser interest in freedom and democracy.

While the influence of Iran and other rogue nations represents the external threat to the prosperity of the Americas, there also continues to be a threat from within.

This is the second challenge I want to identify: the ongoing threat posed by international drug cartels, anti-democratic insurgents, and transnational criminal organizations that have long sought to destabilize Latin America and its democratic nations' economies.

There has been unmistakable progress made in the fight against such lawlessness in Latin America. I witnessed it first-hand this winter.

In Colombia and Mexico, I saw the aggressive, state-of-the-art methods being employed by national police forces in those nations, often using U.S.-built or supplied technology.

Support for U.S. engagement in these vital efforts has traditionally been bipartisan, starting with Plan Colombia, implemented under President Bill Clinton and Speaker Denny Hastert, and the Merida Initiative set in motion by President George W. Bush.

For more than a decade, a major focus of the United States has been to partner with countries whose governments struggle to maintain legitimate state authority over significant portions of their territory.

When our neighbors have faced these situations, we've worked with them to develop, adjust, fund and execute the strategies needed to stem the tide.

These initiatives have been largely successful. But the threat remains.

We know, from years of hard experience, how insurgents, criminal gangs, and terrorist organizations operate when they're left to their own devices.

They form transactional relationships to leverage resources, and create networks for their own survival— carving out zones that allow freedom of movement and operation outside the government's control.

We know such organizations can still spread rapidly in Latin America if left unchecked, partly because of the region's unique characteristics.

The geographical proximity and close cultural connections among the countries, the uneven strengths of the central governments, and other factors lend themselves to a "spillover effec"' in Latin America when such bad actors are given an opening to exploit.

We have to continue to deny them such an opening.

We have an unavoidable responsibility to anticipate this threat and to understand the potential for it to grow as a regional problem in Latin America—one that threatens the smaller countries in the region in particular.

That leads me to the third and most serious challenge, which is the one we don't talk about: the question mark that exists in many of the region's capitals regarding the future of the U.S. commitment.

There are voices in both American political parties calling for the United States to adopt a new posture of isolation and reduce our level of engagement in Latin America, arguing for a halt in aid to nations such as Colombia and Mexico.

The head of the AFL-CIO has called on President Obama to shelve the Colombia Free Trade Agreement.

And the Obama Administration itself, even as it has touted the benefits of free trade with Colombia, has spoken of "turning the page" from Plan Colombia.

The threat of U.S. disengagement is the most serious of the three threats I have identified because if it occurs, the other two threats will multiply exponentially.

This in turn will wipe out economic opportunities —not just for the United States, but for all the nations of our hemisphere.

The vision I have described—a community of nations, committed to free people and free markets—will be in peril.

The best defense against an expansion of Iranian influence in Latin America—and against the destructive aspirations of international criminals in the region—is for the United States to double down on a policy of direct engagement.

The economic potential of Latin America will never be reached if the forces of lawlessness in the region sense that the United States is no longer engaged and committed to their eradication.

For 12 years, Plan Colombia has been the vanguard—the manifestation of the U.S. commitment to a secure, free and prosperous region.

We learned important lessons with it.

We learned that ongoing challenges to the sovereignty of the state were the foundational problem in Colombia.

And we learned the solution required strengthening the state's control of legitimate force, and undercutting the adversaries' ability to use force.

We didn't do everything perfectly with Plan Colombia.

But one point of which we should all be very proud is the special emphasis we placed on training the trainers, which gave our Colombian neighbors the ability to take the lead in providing for their own security.

Colombia still has the second largest insurgency in the world, and we need to take seriously the threat it still poses to the people of Colombia and to the region.

At the same time, there is shared consensus that Colombia has developed training capacity that can be appropriately shared with other like-minded nations in the region.

Rather than drawing down our engagement, the United States should continue to support security assistance and training assistance for Colombia—for continued internal activities, for regional activities, and abroad.

Now is not the time to "turn the page" on Plan Colombia. We need to renew the commitment, and write the next chapter.

There must be no turning of the page until we have worked together to break the back of the threat once and for all.

In both Colombia and Mexico, and the entire hemisphere, the U.S. must be clear that we will not disengage in the fight for free markets and free, secure people.

We must be clear that we will be there, with our friends and partners in the region, committed to fighting and winning the war for a free, stable, and prosperous hemisphere.

We must also be clear about what we expect from all of our neighbors.

We will insist that every nation honor the rule of law, meet its obligations, and respect international norms.

That means paying debts to bondholders; honoring legal commitments and the decisions made by international arbiters; and respecting private property.

Some governments in the region have demonstrated an alarming willingness to drift away from such norms when it suits their objectives.

When this occurs, it's harmful not only to the people of those countries, but to the potential of all of the Americas. And it cannot be excused.

In making speeches, one is always admonished to "know your audience."

I am saying to all the ears in this room—both domestic and international friends—that I am committed to working to ensure this partnership continues, in terms of both policy and resources.

Let me close with an anecdote.

Back in January, when our delegation traveled to Casa de Narino, Colombia's presidential palace, to meet with President Santos, we arrived a bit early.

Having a few minutes to kill, we strolled around Bolívar Square, which had a giant Christmas tree in the center of it and was teeming with people.

A little girl—probably two years old—was walking around the square with her mom, carrying a Mickey Mouse doll.

She dropped the doll as I passed by with my security detail, and I stopped to pick it up for her.

It was just a simple human reflex ... dictated by, if nothing else, manners.

The next morning, in the front section of Colombia's largest newspaper, there's a color photo of the Speaker of the U.S. House in the middle of Bolivar Square picking up a Mickey Mouse doll for a little girl.

I didn't plan that moment, but to me, it was worth a thousand words in describing the relationship we strive for among the neighbor nations of the Western Hemisphere ... a relationship built on fundamental kindness and respect.

My steadfast resolve is to build on the success of the recent past so that one day in the near future, fundamental kindness and respect are attitudes that are taken as 'givens' in these relationships.

We should strive for the kind of relationship in which we're never too busy to stop and help a neighbor— specially a younger one, filled with dreams and potential for the future.

Free markets and free people are the key to a secure, prosperous future for all of the Americas.

It may seem like common sense, but sometimes the most important things are the most obvious ones.

Such is our relationship with Latin America—a relationship vital to the future of our world.

I'm grateful for the opportunity to be with you today. Thank you for listening, and for the honor of this award.

1. How does Speaker Boehner see trade as part of our relationship with Latin America?

2. Based on this speech, what role does politics play in trade?

EXCERPT FROM "REMARKS BY PRESIDENT OBAMA AND PRESIDENT PENA NIETO OF MEXICO IN JOINT PRESS CONFERENCE," FROM THE WHITE HOUSE, JULY 22, 2016

PRESIDENT OBAMA: Good morning, everybody. Buenos dias. Please have a seat. It is always a great pleasure to welcome my good friend and partner, President Peña Nieto of Mexico, to the White House, and his delegation. Enrique and I just worked together at the North American

Leaders Summit in Ottawa last month. Today, we have two of the "Three Amigos"—although the handshake is a little easier when it's just between two people. (Laughter.) ;

Let me start by saying something that is too often overlooked but bears repeating, especially given some of the heated rhetoric that we sometimes hear. The United States values tremendously our enduring partnership with Mexico and our extraordinary ties of family and friendship with the Mexican people.

Mexico is our third-largest trading partner. We sell more to Mexico than we do to China, India, and Russia combined. Every year, millions of tourists and business-people and friends and family cross our border legally. Every day, $1.5 billion in trade and investment crosses our border—and that's trade that supports over a million jobs right here in the United States. On a whole host of issues, from our shared security to climate change, Mexico is a critical partner and is critically important to our own well-being. We're not just strategic and economic partners, we're also neighbors, and we're friends, and we're family —including millions of Americans that are connected to Mexico by ties of culture and of language.

And that's why, as President, I've worked to deepen the partnership between our two nations. And today, Enrique and I discussed ways to keep strengthening the U.S.-Mexico partnership.

First, through forums like our High-Level Economic Dialogue, we're going to keep working to boost trade and grow our economies and create more opportunity for our people. With today's Air Transport Agreement, we're expanding the number of airports that businesses and consumers can fly from, which will make travel and trade more affordable and more efficient. Both our countries are working hard to bring into effect the Trans-Pacific Partnership so that our workers can compete on a level playing field across the Asia Pacific region and can open up doors to new markets.

I reiterated to President Peña Nieto that although I am disappointed in the Supreme Court's failure to come to a decision on our immigration executive action, it is my firm belief that it will be in the interest of the United States —especially our economic interest—to pursue comprehensive immigration reform.

Second, we are deepening our robust partnership on energy and environmental issues. Both of our nations are committed to ensuring that the historic Paris agreement is fully implemented, and we're going to keep on working towards the goal that we announced last month in Ottawa, generating half the electricity in North America through clean power by 2025.

With that goal in mind, we are pursuing an agreement this year on sharing civilian nuclear technology. This fall, our new U.S.-Mexico Energy Business Council will meet for the very first time to strengthen the ties between our energy industries. And, Mr. President, I want to thank you for your vision and your leadership in reforming Mexico's energy industry. I'm also pleased that our nations will continue working to protect our shared ecosystems and environmental heritage.

Third, we'll continue to protect the health and safety of our people—especially from the opioid epidemic that is taking so many lives and devastating so many communities. Both of our nations, we agreed, share a responsibility to combat this crisis. Here in the United States, we're working to improve treatment and prevention, and reduce the availability of illicit drugs. And I applaud President Peña Nieto's commitment to combating organized crime and for developing a new plan to curb poppy cultivation and heroin production. We continue to deploy 21st-century technologies to secure our shared border. And as Mexico makes important reforms to its judicial system, we are working together to strengthen law enforcement and to strengthen observance of human rights and the rule of law.

Fourth, we're stepping up our efforts to tackle regional and global challenges—from confronting cyber threats to fighting diseases like Zika and Dengue. We'll keep partnering with Central American countries to address the instability and poverty that's prompted so many people to embark on the dangerous journey north. And even as we address migration challenges in our own hemisphere, I am very grateful that Mexico is taking an important step on refugee issues and will be co-hosting our Refugee Summit at the United Nations this September.

And finally, we continue to strengthen the strong ties between our people. We want more American students studying in Mexico. We want more Mexican students studying in the United States. So, today, we agreed to extend and update our educational cooperation. Through efforts like our 100,000 Strong in the Americas initiative, we're expanding opportunities for educational exchanges and scientific partnerships and research collaborations. And we're working to help girls learn around the world, including Mexico's commitment to support teachers and schools throughout Latin America and the Caribbean.

In closing, since this is most likely to be our final White House meeting, I'm reminded of what President Peña Nieto said when he first came here almost four years ago. Enrique, you said that our nations had a great opportunity "to have a closer link of brotherhood, of sisterhood, of collaboration and, of course, of great accomplishments." I am proud of what we've achieved together, and proud to stand with you and the Mexican people as our brothers and sisters in progress. And I'm confident that our nations will continue to grow even stronger and more prosperous together in the future.

Muchas gracias. Thank you very much.

PRESIDENT PEÑA NIETO (As interpreted.) Good afternoon, everyone. First of all, I would like to thank President Barack Obama for this very kind invitation to be holding this official visit here at the White House—perhaps the last one that will be taking place here at the White House during your administration, President Obama.

And I would also like to particularly say how important this friendship is, the friendship we have always had from President Obama. And he has been, and his administration, they have been very good neighbors. He has been a very good neighbor and a President committed with the less favored of his country, and with stability also and harmony in our hemisphere, and with a solution of global challenges, as for instance climate change, international migration, and the reduction of nuclear weapons.

I would also like to recognize in his administration the decisive support of favoring migrants, including the over 35 million people of Mexican origin who live in the United States, who are part of the generation of wealth and employment in this country.

I would also like to take advantage of expressing our condolences of the Mexican people, my personal condolences for the lamentable events in Texas and Louisiana.

I fully recognize and acknowledge in President Obama a leader committed in our bilateral relationship, which I should say is today going through one of its best moments and stages in the relationship of the history between our two countries.

In this visit, we have agreed to work on an agenda since 2013, a multi-thematic agenda favoring regional competitiveness. We coincided during our meeting this morning on the importance of institutionalizing accomplishments so that they will be lasting throughout time, with a bilateral forum on higher education. This year, over 64,000 Mexican students will be carrying out academic activities here in the United States.

And on the other hand, the High-Level Economic Dialogue, with the participation of officials of both administrations of the highest-ranking level, has undoubtedly become a platform for integration, competitiveness, and growth. And we have also agreed, ladies and gentlemen, in this meeting to give it a permanent character so that the benefits that derive from this dialogue will be extended throughout time.

Now we have joint cargo inspection programs to reduce costs of up to 50 percent—that is half the cost —and waiting times that have also been reduced by 60 percent. We've also implemented this project, this program at the Laredo, Texas airport, at the Mesa Otay Baja border crossing, and soon this will also be operating in Ciudad Juarez. With projects such as this, we're building a safer, more modern and agile border—a border that undoubtedly generates prosperity for both countries.

Under this framework of competitiveness, we are now celebrating going into effect of the bilateral agreement favoring connectivity between both countries, so that as of the moment this agreement goes into effect, we are going to have more flights—more flights that will be better connecting Mexico and the United States.

And today, we've also formalized the Energy Business Council to support Mexico's transition towards an open and competitive market. And we said that the issues related to security and migration should be analyzed from an internal, comprehensive perspective under the principle of shared responsibility.

We coincide in the fact that consumption and fighting consumption in trafficking heroin is a priority and that we should find solutions to this challenge [...] We have created a high-level task force on drugs focused on heroin and fentanyl.

And we've also decided to increase our cooperation with the governments of Central America, especially Guatemala, El Salvador, and Honduras, so that we can look into migration issues, especially the protection of children that are traveling unaccompanied.

Finally, let me refer to the electoral process that's taking place here in the United States. And let me say that the closeness between the United States and Mexico is more than just a relationship between two governments —it is a solid, a sound, unbreakable relationship among millions of peoples who live in both nations.

And for Mexicans, for Americans, we are all united by 3,000 kilometers of border with neighboring states, -- 10 neighboring states—and a population of over 50 million inhabitants. And their well-being depends on the well-being of their neighbors. And for the Mexican people, for the Mexican government, the very good relationship with the United States of America is, of course, essential.

And from now on and right here, let me express my absolute will of collaboration to whomever is elected in November as the leader of this great nation. The next Madam President or President of the United States will find in Mexico and its government a constructive attitude with proposals and good faith to strengthen the relationship between our two nations.

I am certain, ladies and gentlemen, that the political process in the following months will be characterized by the intensity of the debate and the contrast of ideas, and the vitality of the citizens' participation, according to the great democratic tradition that characterizes the United States. The Mexican government will be observing with great interest the electoral process of this country, but it will not give its opinion. It will not get involved in said process. This is an issue that fully, exclusively corresponds to the people of the United States.

And Mrs. Hillary Clinton and Mr. Donald Trump, I would like to express to both of them my greatest respect, my deepest respect. And from right now, I propose going into a frank, open dialogue with whomever is elected. On the relationship between our two nations, I am sure that with the government of the United States, it will be possible to take a step ahead so that we can face common challenges and take advantage of our enormous opportunities that we share, of course, and find solutions—solutions for possible differences.

Undoubtedly, for Mexico, it is very important for the United States to do well, and for the United States to have a strong economy. And for the United States it's also very convenient for the Mexican economy to also do well. And your next Madam President or President will find in Mexico a strategic partner to face economic security issues that we share, and all the challenges that we share.

I would like to reiterate, President Barack Obama, my appreciation for your hospitality, for this fraternal meeting, for everything—because this is tracing the route and the promise that we can continue working together as sister nations and neighbors. And I reiterate my broadest recognition, President Obama, for being invariably a great friend of Mexico.

Thank you very much.

PRESIDENT OBAMA We've got time for a few questions […].

Q Good afternoon, Mr. Presidents. Both governments have expressed that they are in favor of the free market and globalization. We've heard some voices that oppose themselves to this paradigm. Candidate Trump has pointed out that he is inclined towards protectionism. My question is, do the legal mechanisms of NAFTA provide it with strength so that it is not put aside by decree?

And, President Obama, I'd like to ask you what pending issues you have in your administration that you have liked to complete? Thank you.

PRESIDENT PEÑA NIETO (As interpreted.) I think the free market model of commercial trade openness—this model has undoubtedly shown enormous benefits for nations—for those of us that follow this model, of course. And let me just say that as of the agreement signed with the United States and Canada—I'm talking about NAFTA, of course—the trade level grew over 500 percent—547 percent to be exact—in the last 20 years of NAFTA. And this undoubtedly is reflected in more projected investments, in the creation of jobs, as well. And it has promoted different projects for the development of infrastructure to make our countries even more competitive.

I also think that what is happening is that whenever we've had a slowdown process in the world economy, we start questioning the model, no doubt. However—and this is something I'm fully convinced of—no doubt that this model Mexico has followed and promoted and fostered, well, it has had a particularly important strategic partnership with the U.S. and Canada.

This is a model that still promises a lot of things, so much for the benefits of our citizens, because it allows us to consolidate the North American region as a more competitive region, with a lot more investment, which we are really taking advantage of opportunities to build labor possibilities for our peoples. This is really something we have to highlight and underline.

And bear in mind, because it represents so much and this agreement is projecting into the future, of course —free trade, of course. Right now we can say that this is something that we have had now for 20 years. And I think there are also conditions to modernize, to update, and to find more advantages so that it will potentiate shared common possibilities that we, the three partners, the three strategic partners, have. I am talking about Mexico, the United States, and Canada.

I believe that this agreement, which is also strengthened through TPP, which is now about to be approved in the different countries—undoubtedly they potentialize, they boost, they create a highly promising platform for economic development and for the benefits this will constitute for our societies.

I think the mechanism of solidarity and the purpose—I think the position of the United States is that after 20 years of having NAFTA, we now have eventually the conditions to modernize it, to update NAFTA, and potentialize this agreement even more.

PRESIDENT OBAMA I agree with Enrique that one of the values of the Trans-Pacific Partnership, TPP, is that we've learned from our experience in NAFTA what's worked, what hasn't, where we can strengthen it. And a number of the provisions inside of the Trans-Pacific Partnership address some previous criticisms of NAFTA and will make what is already an extraordinarily strong economic relationship between our two countries even stronger, and will make sure that the process of global integration is serving not just large companies, but is helping small companies and small business and workers.

So what I've said consistently is that globalization is a fact—because of technology, because of an integrated global supply chain, because of changes in transportation. And we're not going to be able to build a wall around that. What we can do is to shape how that process of global integration proceeds so that it's increasing opportunity for ordinary people; so that it's creating better jobs; so that we are strengthening protections for workers; so that we are addressing some of the environmental challenges that come with rapid growth.

And for us to look forward and find ways in which we shape this new direction of the global economy in a way that benefits everybody, rather than to look backwards and think that we can undo what has taken place, I think is our best strategy.

And for all the talk about starting trade wars or increasing protectionist barriers between countries, when you actually examine how our economies work—auto plants in the United States, for example, would have a very hard time producing the number of automobiles they produce—and they've been having record years over the last several years—if they're also not getting some supplies from companies in Mexico. And companies in Mexico are not going to do well if they don't have some connection to not just markets, but also suppliers and technology from the United States.

So we have to focus on how do we ensure the economy works for everybody and not just a few. There are dangers that globalization increased inequality. There are dangers that because capital is mobile and workers are not, if we are not providing them sufficient protection that they can be left behind in this process. And that's what we have to focus on. And the Trans-Pacific Partnership is consistent with that. […]

Q Good afternoon, President. You spoke about the need to institutionalize the agreements reached thus far between both nations. Besides the free trade agreement, which is this agenda of subjects taking into account the change in the administration in the United States? […]

PRESIDENT PEÑA NIETO (As interpreted.) When we speak about institutionalizing mechanisms in both countries, it is for them to be durable throughout time. There are three particularly important mechanisms that undoubtedly are now allowing us to have a very positive, constructive relationship in both nations. First, the High-Level Economic Dialogue—the HLED—that involves the highest-ranking officials of both our administrations that are working in favor of creating a route, a path for infrastructure construction of borders, an infrastructure which is a lot more modern infrastructure that will allow to have more agile trade and commerce between our two nations.

And in terms of security, something that I have already said as many of the other subject matters under responsibility—security cooperation allows us to fight together, jointly, criminal organizations operating in both countries, and maintaining a safe border. All comes from this High-Level Dialogue that we have.

And surely, the academic exchanges—academic exchanges, to seek to have more students from Mexico to be able to come to the United States to get their training, their education here, and North American students to be able to go to Mexico. And this has been a growing impetus. The number of students is 64,000 right now—three years ago it was 15,000—Mexican students who are coming here to study in the United States. This is precisely a decision we decided to continue on this path and to continue promoting it.

And the third thing here is the mechanism to implement innovation, technology, and infrastructure in North America. This is a mechanism that's allowing us to really identify areas of opportunity; to enhance value chains, productive chains, and also supply chains that are there for the production in the United States as well as in Mexico. In fact, we've already defined a clusters mapping process so that we can really promote the economic activity in both nations and how can we strengthen this relationship, of course. And this is another mechanism generated as of the commitment and the will of President Obama's administration.

So the relationship between our two countries is not a monothematic relationship, just focusing on security. But we wanted to really try to launch efforts in both governments to promote competitiveness and productivity of the United States, of Mexico, of North America as a whole, and to really promote and foster this region so that it can become the most attractive region for investments, economic growth and productivity and development. And for that, we have to be working in common fronts, especially in joint projects that are jointly defined that will also allow us to really comply with this purpose and objective.

PRESIDENT OBAMA Let me give a summary of what we mean when we say the need to institutionalize the relationship. I think it's very important to remember that so much of the work that gets done between countries is not done at the level of Presidents, but is done within various agencies—whether it's law enforcement or economic ministries. And when they establish relationships and systems of communications, and shared projects and shared visions, those structures continue even after any particular President is gone, and build trust and understanding between countries that are critically important.

And this gives me a good opportunity I think to emphasize that throughout my presidency, both with

President Peña Nieto and with his predecessor, we have had consistent, strong communications, collaboration. Where there have been differences or tensions, we have consistently tried to work through them in a constructive, positive way.

And to take an example of something that obviously always gets a lot of attention—the issue of the border —a lot of the undocumented workers or migration flows that we've seen over the last several years aren't coming from Mexico but are coming from Central America. And if it were not for the hard work of Mexico in trying to secure its border to the south, and to cooperate with us, we would have a much more significant problem.

And that's not always easy. That requires resources and policy decisions made by the Mexican government. But the cooperation on that front has been absolutely critical in making sure that we deal with these issues in a serious way and in a humane way. And we continue to make progress on that front.

The same is true when it comes to drug trafficking. This is a problem in both of our countries. And as a consequence of the work that we've done together, we have seen progress in some areas, both in the flow of drugs north, but also in the flow of guns and illicit financing south. But we're not going to be able to solve this problem by ourselves. And Mexico is going to need the United States to cooperate in order to rid itself of the violence and corruption that results from the drug trade.

And so the more we can build these kinds of habits of cooperation and engrain them in our various agencies, the better off we're going to be. And I want everybody to be very clear Mexico has been a consistent, strong partner with us on these issues. And if they had not been, we would have had much bigger problems on our borders. And the benefit of a cooperative Mexico—and, by the way, a Mexico that has a healthy economy, a Mexico that can help us build stability and security in Central America—that's going to do a lot more to solve any migration crisis or drug trafficking problem than a wall. And it will be much more reflective of the kind of relationship that we should have with our neighbors.

Mr. President, thank you.

PRESIDENT PEÑA NIETO Thank you. Thank you so much.

1. How has NAFTA changed trade between the United States and Mexico? What are some of the positives and negatives suggested here?

2. What are other issues that trade helps to address?

"WANT TO HELP FREE TRADE'S LOSERS? MAKE 'ADJUSTMENT ASSISTANCE' MORE THAN JUST BURIAL INSURANCE," BY MARINA V. N. WHITMAN, FROM *THE CONVERSATION* WITH THE PARTNERSHIP OF THE UNIVERSITY OF MICHIGAN, OCTOBER 24, 2016

If there's one thing that nearly all economists agree on, it's that getting rid of trade restrictions is generally good for a country's economy.

Doing so leads to a higher national income, faster economic growth, higher productivity and more competition and innovation. Freer trade also tends to lower prices and improve the quality of the goods that are particularly important in the budgets of poorer families.

But you certainly wouldn't know it from the current political landscape. Hillary Clinton has repudiated the Trans-Pacific Partnership (TPP) she once hailed as the gold standard of trade deals. Donald Trump would go much further and not only tear up the North American Free Trade Agreement (NAFTA) but consider withdrawing from the World Trade Organization (WTO) as well.

So what has made free trade—which still gets the support of most Americans—such a political pariah?

A major explanation is that there are losers as well as winners from its effects. The winners may be far more numerous, yet the impact on the losers, from lost jobs and lower wages, is more intense and personal.

I've been a steady and vocal proponent of the view that freer trade's benefits far outweigh its costs. When the former president of the United Auto Workers, Owen Bieber, called me "that free-trade bitch at GM" in the early 1990s, I took it as a compliment. While I still believe the research (mine included) supports lowering restrictions on trade, we haven't called enough attention to the "losers," partly because we underestimated how much they'd be hurt.

WHERE LIBERALIZING TRADE WENT WRONG

Both Trump and Bernie Sanders have made opposition to freer trade key to their platforms, often citing the loss of over 4.5 million manufacturing jobs since 1994.

Recent research indicates that China's unforeseen emergence in the 1990s as a global competitor in the world markets can be blamed for at least 20 percent of that, significantly more than earlier estimates.

A just-published paper that estimates the effects of NAFTA on blue-collar workers, not only in goods industries but service industries as well, found similar results. Particularly vulnerable were the footwear and oil and gas industries and the states of North and South Carolina.

Both studies suggest that the American labor market is not as fluid and flexible as we thought. Job losers were not able to find new ones as quickly as expected nor command the same level of wages when they did. This finding is consistent with other research indicating that the in-country mobility of blue-collar American workers has been falling.

In other words, while the overall welfare effects of trade liberalization are generally positive, the impact on some subgroups, particularly the less well-educated, are negative and much larger.

And the United States is less generous than other rich countries in providing both reemployment assistance and income support to workers hurt by these changes.

The primary U.S. program aimed at mitigating this negative impact is known as trade adjustment assistance (TAA). That its intended recipients call it "burial insurance" sort of sums up its image problem.

SOFTENING THE BLOW OF FREE TRADE

Trade adjustment assistance has gone through a variety of forms since its origins in the 1950s, but today it provides displaced workers with relocation assistance, subsidized health insurance and extended unemployment benefits. A typical condition of aid is that recipients have to enroll in a job training program.

The idea came in 1954, when the head of the Steelworkers Union first suggested helping workers adversely affected by imports. Eight years later, Congress turned the idea into law as a crucial carrot to win the backing of the AFL-CIO for the Trade Expansion Act, which gave the president the unilateral authority to cut many tariffs by up to 50 percent over a five-year period.

All the aid provision did, however, was provide workers with temporary and severely delayed supplements to their unemployment compensation. It was little used because the eligibility requirements were so strict.

The TAA program was formally established as part of the Trade Act of 1974, which created the so-called "fast-track" process limiting Congress to a simple up-or-down vote on negotiated trade deals and set up a permanent trade office. The program eased eligibility requirements, specifying only that "imports contributed importantly" to a job loss, and offered expanded unemployment insurance. As a result, the number of petitions under the program surged, mainly from the auto, steel, textile and apparel industries, and most were certified for payment.

Despite this, the trade assistance earned the epithet "burial insurance" by many in the labor movement. As a Republican senator put it in 1978:

> "Adjustment assistance has often been scornfully, but accurately, called burial assistance—arriving only in time to dispose of the victim."

Ronald Reagan put the program high on his hit list when he became president in 1981. The size of individual payments was reduced and capped at 52 weeks, joining a training program became a requirement for aid. And far fewer petitioners received aid.

TAA LIMPS ON

Over subsequent years the program (including various offshoots) grew and shrunk but continued to be used primarily to win congressional authorization of various trade agreements.

The Clinton administration created NAFTA-Transitional Adjustment Assistance—for those who lost jobs, hours or wages due to increased imports from or shifts of production to Mexico or Canada—to win labor votes for the North American trade deal.

That helped NAFTA win narrow approval in 1993, but the main result of the new program was overlap and confusion with the original and led to declining support for free trade throughout the '90's.

President George W. Bush reformed the assistance programs as he tried to muster support for a new round of trade negotiations early in his first term. The Trade Act of 2002 eliminated NAFTA-TAA as a separate program, reauthorized the fast-track process and established a health tax credit and partial wage insurance for older, lower-paid displaced workers who found new jobs but at less pay than the old ones.

These changes—which made TAA the most generous and expensive it's ever been—failed to satisfy organized labor, which still tended to see the program as burial insurance and unable to make up for the loss of "good manufacturing jobs." A study commissioned by Congress concluded that workers who took trade assistance fared no better, in terms of employment and earnings, than those who got regular unemployment insurance.

Another big change came in 2009 when for the first time trade assistance was reauthorized on its own, rather than in conjunction with other trade initiatives, as part of the American Recovery and Reinvestment Act. It expanded the program, most notably by extending it to service sector workers.

Since then, it has been reauthorized several times, usually as part of a trade package. Most recently, a 2015 bill restored fast-track for President Barack Obama—aimed at helping him seal the TPP trade deal he was working on — and also reauthorized the TAA program through 2022, but included "sunset" provisions.

RETHINKING TRADE ADJUSTMENT ASSISTANCE

The TPP, which was agreed to earlier this year by 12 Pacific Rim countries, is aimed at reducing tariffs but, much more significantly, it would remove other national barriers to finance and investment as well as trade in goods, services and digital transactions. Among these changes are harmonization of national regulations and protection of intellectual property.

That agreement, which still requires ratification by the Senate, is now on the rocks after the populist candidacies of Trump and Sanders seized on anti-trade sentiment and gave it a powerful voice.

While this won't save the TPP, rethinking how we assist those hurt by free trade is important so that at a minimum —once the anti-globalization views now ascendant have attenuated and the U.S. budget can accommodate increases in discretionary programs—future agreements don't leave so many workers feeling left behind. Tinkering isn't enough.

It starts with crafting policies that encourage a more flexible labor force, while at the same time providing a safety net for those who have to do the flexing. The Danes have coined a word for such policies: "flexicurity." Rather than trying to protect jobs toppled by economist Joseph Schumpeter's "winds of creative destruction," government policies should ease and speed the transition to new and sturdier ones.

So in terms of the TAA, a crucial change would be to make training and other programs for the reemployment of displaced workers more effective and wage insurance for those who have found new jobs but at significantly lower salaries than the old ones more generous, in both amounts and duration. It is also critical to extend such measures to all workers displaced by change—such automation and changes in consumers' tastes—not just trade.

Marketing will also have to play a role, from changing the name to delinking such provisions from political horse-trading over trade deals.

That way, perhaps government assistance for the losers from free trade could be thought of as something that lifts them up rather than puts them in the ground.

1. How can trade adjustment assistance (TAA) help make free trade more equitable?

2. How have politicians changed their views on free trade in recent years?

CHAPTER 3

WHAT THE COURTS SAY

Court decisions on trade deals are rare, but they do occur. In a historical overview of important court decisions on trade deals in the 1930s and 1940s, Richard M. Ebeling examines the Supreme Court's role in establishing "economic freedom" and fighting against "economic fascism." Today, cases based in trade agreements are often tied to specific business concerns or the delegation of powers within the government, as is the case in *Crosby v. National Foreign Trade Council* (2000). In this important case, the US Supreme Court determined that the state of Massachusetts could not implement the so-called Burma Law, which prohibited the state's governmental agencies from buying products from Myanmar (Burma) because of human rights abuses committed in that country. The unanimous decision, reproduced below, found that Massachusetts was preempting federal trade sanctions on Myanmar and, thus, could not stand. Although these kinds of cases are not heard often, they play an important role in shaping how trade policy is implemented, including how free trade agreements can be held accountable to businesses and individuals.

"WHEN THE SUPREME COURT STOPPED ECONOMIC FASCISM IN AMERICA," BY RICHARD M. EBELING, FROM THE FOUNDATION FOR ECONOMIC EDUCATION, OCTOBER 1, 2005

Seventy years ago, on May 27, 1935, the U.S. Supreme Court said no to economic fascism in America. The trend toward bigger and ever-more intrusive government, unfortunately, was not stopped, but the case nonetheless was a significant event that at that time prevented the institutionalizing of a Mussolini-type corporativist system in America.

In a unanimous decision the nine members of the Supreme Court said there were constitutional limits beyond which the federal government could not go in claiming the right to regulate the economic affairs of the citizenry. It was a glorious day in American judicial history, and is worth remembering.

When Franklin Roosevelt ran for president in the autumn of 1932 he did so on a Democratic Party platform that many a classical liberal might have gladly supported and even voted for. The platform said that the federal government was far too big, taxed and spent far too much, and intruded in the affairs of the states to too great an extent. It said government spending had to be cut, taxes reduced, and the federal budget balanced. It called for free trade and a solid gold-backed currency.

But as soon as Roosevelt took office in March 1933 he instituted a series of programs and policies that turned all those promises upside down. In the first four years of FDR's New Deal, taxes were increased, government spending reached heights never seen before in U.S. history, and the federal budget bled red with deficits.The bureaucracy ballooned; public-works projects increasingly dotted the land; and the heavy hand of government was all over industry and agriculture. The United States was taken off the gold standard, with the American people compelled to turn in their gold com and built lion to the government for paper money under the threat of confiscation and imprisonment.

In June 1933 Congress passed the National Industrial Recovery Act (NIRA), after which FDR created the National Recovery Administration (NRA). Modeled on Mussolini's fascist economic system, it forced virtually all American industry, manufacturing, and retail business into cartels possessing the power to set prices and wages, and to dictate the levels of production. Within a few months over 200 separate pricing and production codes were imposed on the various branches of American business. The symbol of the NRA was a Blue Eagle that had lightning bolts in one claw and an industrial gear in the other. Every business in the country was asked to have a Blue Eagle sign in its window that declared, "We Do Our Part," meaning it followed the pricing and production codes. Citizen committees were formed to spy on local merchants and report if they dared to sell at lower prices.

Propaganda rallies in support of the NRA were held across the country. During halftime at football games cheerleaders would form the shape of the Blue Eagle. Government-sponsored parades featured Hollywood stars supporting the NRA. At one of these parades the famous singer Al Jolson was filmed being asked what he thought of the NRA; he replied, "NRA? NRA? Why it's better than my wedding night!" Film shorts produced by Hollywood in support of the NRA were shown in theaters around the country; in one of them child star Shirley Temple danced and sang the praises of big-government regulation of the American economy.

The NRA codes were soon joined by similar controls over farming with the passage of the Agricultural Adjustment Act (AAA). Farmers were given subsidies and government-guaranteed price supports, with Washington determining what crops could be grown and what livestock could be raised. Government ordered some crops to be plowed under and some live-stock slaughtered, all in the name of centrally planned farm production and pricing.

Much of the urban youth of America were rounded up and sent off to national forests for regi-mentation and mock military-style drilling as part of the Civilian Conservation Corps (CCC). The Works Progress Administration (WPA) created make-work projects for thousands of able-bodied men, all at taxpayers' expense. Since unemployed artists were "workers" too, they were set to work in government buildings across the land. Even today, in some of the post offices dating from the 1930s, one can see murals depicting happy factory workers and farm hands in a style similar to those produced in Stalin's Russia and Hitler's Germany.

This headlong march into economic fascism was brought to a halt by the Supreme Court. The catalyst was a legal case known as the *Schechter Poultry Corp. v. United States*. Schechter, a slaughterhouse that sold chickens to kosher markets in New York City, was accused of violating the "fair competition" codes under the NRA. The case made its way up to the Supreme Court, with the nine justices laying down their unanimous decision on May 27, 1935.

Three hundred people packed the court that day to hear the decision, with prominent members of Congress and the executive branch in the audience. The justices declared that the federal government had exceeded its authority under the interstate-commerce clause of the Constitution, since the defendant purchased and sold all the chickens it marketed within the boundaries of the State of New York. Therefore, the federal government lacked the power to regulate the company's production and prices. In addition, the justices stated that the NRA's power to impose codes constituted arbitrary and discretionary control inconsistent with the limited and enumerated powers delegated by the Constitution.

AAA REJECTED

This was soon followed by the Supreme Court's rejection of the AAA in January 1936, when the justices insisted that the federal government lacked the authority to tax food processors to pay for the farmers' subsidies and price supports. Furthermore, since farming was generally a local and state activity, the federal government did not have the power to regulate it under the interstate-commerce clause.

Franklin Roosevelt was furious that what he called those "nine old men" should attempt to keep America in the "horse and buggy era" when this great nation needed a more powerful central government to manage economic affairs in the "modern age." FDR's response was his famous "court packing" scheme, in which he asked

Congress to give him the power to add more justices to the Supreme Court in order to tilt the balance in favor of the "enlightened" and "progressive" policies of the New Deal. But this blatant power grab by the executive branch ended up being too much even for many of the Democrats in Congress, and Roosevelt failed in this attempt to assert naked presidential authority over another branch o f the federal government.

Shortly after the Supreme Court declared both the NRA and AAA unconstitutional, David Lawrence, founder and long-time editor of *U.S. News and World Report*, published a book titled *Nine Honest Men* (1936). He praised the justices for their devotion to the bedrock principles of the Constitution, and their defense of the traditional American ideals of individual liberty, private property, and the rule of law—even in the face of the emotional appeal of government to "do something" during an economic crisis.

Since that landmark decision 70 years ago against the imposition of economic fascism in America, the U.S. government has continued to grow in power over the American citizenry. But it should be remembered that men of courage, integrity, and principle can stand up to Big Brother and resist the headlong march into economic tyranny.

1. What do you think about this historical analysis of important trade decisions in the courts in the 1930s and 1940s? Do you agree with the author's analysis?

2. Do you think the author is right to use the term "fascism" in this sense? Why or why not?

EXCERPT FROM *STEPHEN P. CROSBY, SECRETARY OF ADMINISTRATION AND FINANCE OF MASSACHUSETTS, ET AL., V. NATIONAL FOREIGN TRADE COUNCIL*, FROM THE UNITED STATES SUPREME COURT, JUNE 19, 2000

Justice Souter delivered the opinion of the Court.

The issue is whether the Burma law of the Commonwealth of Massachusetts, restricting the authority of its agencies to purchase goods or services from companies doing business with Burma,[1] is invalid under the Supremacy Clause of the National Constitution owing to its threat of frustrating federal statutory objectives. We hold that it is.

I

In June 1996, Massachusetts adopted "An Act Regulating State Contracts with Companies Doing Business with or in Burma (Myanmar)," 1996 Mass. Acts 239, ch. 130 (codified at Mass. Gen. Laws §§7:22G-7:22M, 40 F½ (1997). The statute generally bars state entities from buying goods or services from any person (defined to include a business organization) identified on a "restricted purchase list" of those doing business with Burma. §§7:22H(a), 7:22J. Although the statute has no general provision for waiver or termination of its ban, it does exempt from boycott any entities present in Burma solely to report the news, §7:22H(e), or to provide international telecommunication goods or services, *ibid.*, or medical supplies, §7:22I.

" `Doing business with Burma' " is defined broadly to cover any person

"(a) having a principal place of business, place of incorporation or its corporate headquarters in Burma (Myanmar) or having any operations, leases, franchises, majority-owned subsidiaries, distribution agreements, or any other similar agreements in Burma (Myanmar), or being the majority-owned subsidiary, licensee or franchise of such a person;

"(b) providing financial services to the government of Burma (Myanmar), including providing direct loans, underwriting government securities, providing any consulting advice or assistance, providing brokerage services, acting as a trustee or escrow agent, or otherwise acting as an agent pursuant to a contractual agreement;

"(c) promoting the importation or sale of gems, timber, oil, gas or other related products, commerce in which is largely controlled by the government of Burma (Myanmar), from Burma (Myanmar);

"(d) providing any goods or services to the government of Burma (Myanmar)." §7:22G.

There are three exceptions to the ban: (1) if the procurement is essential, and without the restricted bid, there would be no bids or insufficient competition, §7:22H(b); (2) if the procurement is of medical supplies, §7:22I; and (3) if the procurement efforts elicit no "comparable low bid or offer" by a person not doing business with Burma, §7:22H(d), meaning an offer that is no more than 10 percent greater than the restricted bid, §7:22G. To enforce the ban, the Act requires petitioner Secretary of Administration and Finance to maintain a "restricted purchase list" of all firms "doing business with Burma,"[2] §7:22J.

In September 1996, three months after the Massachusetts law was enacted, Congress passed a statute imposing a set of mandatory and conditional sanctions on Burma. See Foreign Operations, Export Financing, and Related Programs Appropriations Act, 1997, §570, 110 Stat. 3009-166 to 3009-167 (enacted by the Omnibus Consolidated Appropriations Act, 1997, §101(c), 110 Stat. 3009-121 to 3009-172). The federal Act has five basic parts, three substantive and two procedural.

First, it imposes three sanctions directly on Burma. It bans all aid to the Burmese Government except for humanitarian assistance, counternarcotics efforts, and promotion of human rights and democracy. §570(a)(1). The statute instructs United States representatives to international financial institutions to vote against loans or other assistance to or for Burma, §570(a)(2), and it provides that no entry visa shall be issued to any Burmese government official unless required by treaty or to staff the Burmese mission to the United Nations, §570(a)(3). These restrictions are to remain in effect "[u]ntil such time as the President determines and certifies to Congress that Burma has made measurable and substantial progress in improving human rights practices and implementing democratic government." §570(a).

Second, the federal Act authorizes the President to impose further sanctions subject to certain conditions. He may prohibit "United States persons" from "new investment" in Burma, and shall do so if he determines and certifies to Congress that the Burmese Government has physically harmed, rearrested, or exiled Daw Aung San Suu Kyi (the opposition leader selected to receive the Nobel Peace Prize), or has committed "large-scale repression of or violence against the Democratic opposition." §570(b). "New investment" is defined as entry into a contract that would favor the "economical development of resources located in Burma," or would provide ownership interests in or benefits from such development, §570(f)(2), but the term specifically excludes (and thus excludes from any Presidential prohibition) "entry into, performance of, or financing of a contract to sell or purchase goods, services, or technology," *ibid*.

Third, the statute directs the President to work to develop "a comprehensive, multilateral strategy to bring democracy to and improve human rights practices and the quality of life in Burma." §570(c). He is instructed to cooperate with members of the Association of Southeast Asian Nations (ASEAN) and with other countries having major trade and investment interests in Burma to devise such an approach, and to pursue the additional objective of fostering dialogue between the ruling State Law and Order Restoration Council (SLORC) and democratic opposition groups. *Ibid.*

As for the procedural provisions of the federal statute, the fourth section requires the President to report periodically to certain congressional committee chairmen on the progress toward democratization and better living conditions in Burma as well as on the development of the required strategy. §570(d). And the fifth part of the federal Act authorizes the President "to waive, temporarily or permanently, any sanction [under the federal Act] ... if he determines and certifies to Congress that the application of such sanction would be contrary to the national security interests of the United States." §570(e).

On May 20, 1997, the President issued the Burma Executive Order, Exec. Order No. 13047, 3 CFR 202 (1997 Comp.). He certified for purposes of §570(b) that the Government of Burma had "committed large-scale repression of the democratic opposition in Burma" and found that the Burmese Government's actions and policies constituted "an unusual and extraordinary threat to the national security and foreign policy of the United States," a threat characterized as a national emergency. The President then prohibited new investment in Burma "by United States persons," Exec. Order No. 13047, §1, any approval or facilitation by a United States person of such new investment by foreign persons, §2(a), and any transaction meant to evade or avoid the ban, §2(b). The order generally incorporated the exceptions and exemptions addressed in the statute. §§3, 4. Finally, the President delegated to the Secretary of State the tasks of working with ASEAN and other countries to develop a strategy for democracy, human rights, and the quality of life in Burma, and of making the required congressional reports.[3] §5.

II

Respondent National Foreign Trade Council (Council) is a nonprofit corporation representing companies engaged in foreign commerce; 34 of its members were on the Massachusetts restricted purchase list in 1998. [...] Three withdrew from Burma after the passage of the state Act, and one member had its bid for a procurement contract increased by 10 percent under the provision of the state law allowing acceptance of a low bid from a listed bidder only if the next-to-lowest bid is more than 10 percent higher. *Ibid.*

In April 1998, the Council filed suit in the United States District Court for the District of Massachusetts, seeking declaratory and injunctive relief against the petitioner state officials charged with administering and enforcing the state Act (whom we will refer to simply as the State).[4] The Council argued that the state law unconstitutionally infringed on the federal foreign affairs power, violated the Foreign Commerce Clause, and was preempted by the federal Act. After detailed stipulations, briefing, and argument, the District Court permanently enjoined enforcement of the state Act, holding that it "unconstitutionally impinge[d] on the federal government's exclusive authority to regulate foreign affairs." [...]

The United States Court of Appeals for the First Circuit affirmed on three independent grounds. 181 F. 3d, at 45. It found the state Act unconstitutionally interfered with the foreign affairs power of the National Government under *Zschernig v. Miller*, 389 U. S. 429 (1968), see 181 F. 3d, at 52-55; violated the dormant Foreign Commerce Clause, U. S. Const. Art. I, §8, cl. 3, see 181 F. 3d, at 61-71; and was preempted by the congressional Burma Act, see *id.*, at 71-77.

The State's petition for certiorari challenged the decision on all three grounds and asserted interests said to be shared by other state and local governments with similar measures.[5] Though opposing certiorari, the Council acknowledged the significance of the issues and the need to settle the constitutionality of such laws and regulations. Brief in Opposition 18-19. We granted certiorari to resolve these important questions, 528 U. S. 1018 (1999), and now affirm.

III

A fundamental principle of the Constitution is that Congress has the power to preempt state law. [...] Even without an express provision for preemption, we have found that state law must yield to a congressional Act in at least two circumstances. When Congress intends federal law to "occupy the field," state law in that area is preempted. [...] And even if Congress has not occupied the field, state law is naturally preempted to the extent of any conflict with a federal statute.[6] [...] We will find preemption where it is impossible for a private party to comply with both state and federal law, [...] and where "under the circumstances of [a] particular case, [the challenged state law] stands as an obstacle to the accomplishment and execution of the full purposes and objectives of Congress." [...] What is a sufficient obstacle is a matter of judgment, to be informed by examining the federal statute as a whole and identifying its purpose and intended effects:

> "For when the question is whether a Federal act overrides a state law, the entire scheme of the statute must of course be considered and that which needs must be implied is of no less force than that which is expressed. If the purpose of the act cannot otherwise be accomplished--if its operation within its chosen field else must be frustrated and its provisions be refused their natural effect--the state law must yield to the regulation of Congress within the sphere of its delegated power." *Savage*, supra, 533, quoted in *Hines*, *supra*, at 67, n. 20.

Applying this standard, we see the state Burma law as an obstacle to the accomplishment of Congress's full objectives under the federal Act.[7] We find that the state law undermines the intended purpose and "natural effect" of at least three provisions of the federal Act, that is, its delegation of effective discretion to the President to control economic sanctions against Burma, its limitation of sanctions solely to United States persons and new investment, and its directive to the President to proceed diplomatically in developing a comprehensive, multilateral strategy towards Burma.[8]

A

First, Congress clearly intended the federal act to provide the President with flexible and effective authority over economic sanctions against Burma. Although Congress immediately put in place a set of initial sanctions (prohibiting bilateral aid, §570(a)(1), support for international financial assistance, §570(a)(2), and entry by Burmese officials into the United States, §570(a)(3)), it authorized the President to terminate any and all of those measures upon determining and certifying that there had been progress in human rights and democracy in Burma. §570(a). It invested the President with the further power to ban new investment by United States persons, dependent only on specific Presidential findings of repression in Burma. §570(b). And, most significantly, Congress empowered the President "to waive, temporarily or permanently, any sanction [under the federal act] ... if he determines and certifies to Congress that the application of such sanction would be contrary to the national security interests of the United States." §570(e).

This express investiture of the President with statutory authority to act for the United States in imposing sanctions with respect to the government of Burma, augmented by the flexibility[9] to respond to change by suspending sanctions in the interest of national security, recalls Justice Jackson's observation in *Youngstown Sheet & Tube Co. v. Sawyer*, 343 U. S. 579, 635 (1952): "When the President acts pursuant to an express or implied authorization of Congress, his authority is at its maximum, for it includes all that he possesses in his own right plus all that Congress can delegate." See also *id.*, at 635-636, n. 2 (noting that the President's power in the area of foreign relations is least restricted by Congress and citing *United States v. Curtiss-Wright Export Corp.*, 299 U. S. 304 (1936)). Within the sphere defined by Congress, then, the statute has placed the President in a position with as much discretion to exercise economic leverage against Burma, with an eye toward national security, as our law will admit. And it is just this plenitude of Executive authority that we think controls the issue of preemption here. The President has been given this authority not merely to make a political statement but to achieve a political result, and the fullness of his authority shows the importance in the congressional mind of reaching that result. It is simply implausible that Congress would have gone to such lengths to empower the President if it had been willing to compromise his effectiveness by deference to every provision of state statute or local ordinance that might, if enforced, blunt the consequences of discretionary Presidential action.[10]

And that is just what the Massachusetts Burma law would do in imposing a different, state system of economic pressure against the Burmese political regime. As will be seen, the state statute penalizes some private action that the federal Act (as administered by the President) may allow, and pulls levers of influence that the federal Act does not reach. But the point here is that the state sanctions are immediate,[11] see 1996 Mass. Acts 239, ch. 130, §3 (restricting all contracts after law's effective date); Mass. Gen Laws §7:22K (1997) (authorizing regulations for timely and effective implementation), and perpetual, there being no termination provision, see, *e.g.*, §7:22J (restricted companies list to be updated at least every three months). This unyielding application undermines the President's intended statutory authority by making it impossible for him to restrain fully the coercive power of the national economy when he may choose to take the discretionary action open to him, whether he believes that the national interest requires sanctions to be lifted, or believes that the promise of lifting sanctions would move the Burmese regime in the democratic direction. Quite simply, if the Massachusetts law is enforceable the President has less to offer and less economic and diplomatic leverage as a consequence. In *Dames & Moore v. Regan*, 453 U. S. 654 (1981), we used the metaphor of the bargaining chip to describe the President's control of funds valuable to a hostile country, *id.*, at 673; here, the state Act reduces the value of the chips created by the federal statute.[12] It thus "stands as an obstacle to the accomplishment and execution of the full purposes and objectives of Congress." *Hines*, 312 U. S., at 67.

B

Congress manifestly intended to limit economic pressure against the Burmese Government to a specific range. The federal Act confines its reach to United States persons,

§570(b), imposes limited immediate sanctions, §570(a), places only a conditional ban on a carefully defined area of "new investment," §570(f)(2), and pointedly exempts contracts to sell or purchase goods, services, or technology, §570(f)(2). These detailed provisions show that Congress's calibrated Burma policy is a deliberate effort "to steer a middle path," id. at 73.[13]

The State has set a different course, and its statute conflicts with federal law at a number of points by penalizing individuals and conduct that Congress has explicitly exempted or excluded from sanctions. While the state Act differs from the federal in relying entirely on indirect economic leverage through third parties with Burmese connections, it otherwise stands in clear contrast to the congressional scheme in the scope of subject matter addressed. It restricts all contracts between the State and companies doing business in Burma, §7:22H(a), except when purchasing medical supplies and other essentials (or when short of comparable bids), §7:22I. It is specific in targeting contracts to provide financial services, §7:22G(b), and general goods and services, §7:22G(d), to the Government of Burma, and thus prohibits contracts between the State and United States persons for goods, services, or technology, even though those transactions are explicitly exempted from the ambit of new investment prohibition when the President exercises his discretionary authority to impose sanctions under the federal Act. §570(f)(2).

As with the subject of business meant to be affected, so with the class of companies doing it: the state Act's generality stands at odds with the federal discreteness. The Massachusetts law directly and indirectly imposes costs on all companies that do any business in

Burma, §7:22G, save for those reporting news or providing international telecommunications goods or services, or medical supplies, §§7:22H(e), 7:22I. It sanctions companies promoting the importation of natural resources controlled by the government of Burma, or having any operations or affiliates in Burma. §7:22G. The state Act thus penalizes companies with pre-existing affiliates or investments, all of which lie beyond the reach of the federal act's restrictions on "new investment" in Burmese economic development. §§570(b), 570(f)(2). The state Act, moreover, imposes restrictions on foreign companies as well as domestic, whereas the federal Act limits its reach to United States persons.

The conflicts are not rendered irrelevant by the State's argument that there is no real conflict between the statutes because they share the same goals and because some companies may comply with both sets of restrictions. See Brief for Petitioners 21-22. The fact of a common end hardly neutralizes conflicting means,[14] see *Gade v. National Solid Wastes Management Assn.*, 505 U. S. 88, 103 (1992), and the fact that some companies may be able to comply with both sets of sanctions does not mean that the state Act is not at odds with achievement of the federal decision about the right degree of pressure to employ. […] Sanctions are drawn not only to bar what they prohibit but to allow what they permit, and the inconsistency of sanctions here undermines the congressional calibration of force.

C

Finally, the state Act is at odds with the President's intended authority to speak for the United States among the world's nations in developing a "comprehensive, multilateral strategy to bring democracy to and improve human rights practices and the quality of life in Burma." §570(c). Congress called for Presidential cooperation with members of ASEAN and other countries in developing such a strategy, *ibid.*, directed the President to encourage a dialogue between the government of Burma and the democratic opposition, *ibid.*,15 and required him to report to the Congress on the progress of his diplomatic efforts, §570(d). As with Congress's explicit delegation to the President of power over economic sanctions, Congress's express command to the President to take the initiative for the United States among the international community invested him with the maximum authority of the National Government, cf. *Youngstown Sheet & Tube Co.*, 343 U. S., at 635, in harmony with the President's own constitutional powers, U. S. Const., Art. II, §2, cl. 2 ("[The President] shall have Power, by and with the Advice and Consent of the Senate, to make Treaties" and "shall appoint Ambassadors, other public Ministers and Consuls"); §3 ("[The President] shall receive Ambassadors and other public Ministers"). This clear mandate and invocation of exclusively national power belies any suggestion that Congress intended the President's effective voice to be obscured by state or local action.

Again, the state Act undermines the President's capacity, in this instance for effective diplomacy. It is not merely that the differences between the state and federal Acts in scope and type of sanctions threaten to complicate discussions; they compromise the very capacity of the President to speak for the Nation with one voice in dealing with other governments. We need not get into any general consideration of limits of state action affecting foreign affairs to realize that the President's maximum power to persuade rests on his capacity to bargain for the benefits of access to the entire national economy without exception for enclaves fenced off willy-nilly by inconsistent political tactics.[16] When such exceptions do qualify his capacity to present a coherent position on behalf of the national economy, he is weakened, of course, not only in dealing with the Burmese regime, but in working together with other nations in hopes of reaching common policy and "comprehensive" strategy.[17] Cf. *Dames & Moore*, 453 U. S., at 673-674.

While the threat to the President's power to speak and bargain effectively with other nations seems clear enough, the record is replete with evidence to answer any skeptics. First, in response to the passage of the state Act, a number of this country's allies and trading partners filed formal protests with the National Government, see 181 F. 3d, at 47 (noting protests from Japan, the European Union (EU), and ASEAN), including an official *Note Verbale* from the EU to the Department of State protesting the state Act.[18] EU officials have warned that the state Act "could have a damaging effect on bilateral EU-US relations." Hugo Paemen, Ambassador, European Union, Delegation of the European Commission, to William F. Weld, Governor, State of Massachusetts, Jan. 23, 1997, App. 75.

Second, the EU and Japan have gone a step further in lodging formal complaints against the United States in the World Trade Organization (WTO), claiming that the state Act violates certain provisions of the Agreement on Government Procurement,[19] H. R. Doc. No. 103-316, 1719 (1994) and the consequence has been to embroil the

National Government for some time now in international dispute proceedings under the auspices of the WTO. In their brief before this Court, EU officials point to the WTO dispute as threatening relations with the United States, Brief for European Communities et al. as *Amici Curiae* 7, and n. 7, and note that the state Act has become the topic of "intensive discussions" with officials of the United States at the highest levels, those discussions including exchanges at the twice yearly EU-U. S. Summit.[20]

    Third, the Executive has consistently represented that the state Act has complicated its dealings with foreign sovereigns and proven an impediment to accomplishing objectives assigned it by Congress. Assistant Secretary of State Larson, for example, has directly addressed the mandate of the federal Burma law in saying that the imposition of unilateral state sanctions under the state Act "complicates efforts to build coalitions with our allies" to promote democracy and human rights in Burma. A. Larson, State and Local Sanctions: Remarks to the Council of State Governments 5 (Dec. 8, 1998). "[T]he EU's opposition to the Massachusetts law has meant that U. S. government high level discussions with EU officials often have focused not on what to do about Burma, but on what to do about the Massachusetts Burma law." *Id.*, at 3.[21] This point has been consistently echoed in the State Department:

> "While the [Massachusetts sanctions on Burma] were adopted in pursuit of a noble goal, the restoration of democracy in Burma, these measures also risk shifting the focus of the debate with our European Allies away from the best way to bring pressure against the State Law and Order Restoration Council (SLORC) to a potential WTO dispute over its

consistency with our international obligations. Let me be clear. We are working with Massachusetts in the WTO dispute settlement process. But we must be honest in saying that the threatened WTO case risks diverting United States' and Europe's attention from focusing where it should be--on Burma." Eizenstat testimony, App. 115.[22]

This evidence in combination is more than sufficient to show that the state Act stands as an obstacle in addressing the congressional obligation to devise a comprehensive, multilateral strategy.

Our discussion in *Barclays Bank PLC v. Franchise Tax Bd. of Cal.*, 512 U. S. 298, 327-329 (1994), of the limited weight of evidence of formal diplomatic protests, risk of foreign retaliation, and statements by the Executive does not undercut the point. In *Barclays*, we had the question of the preemptive effect of federal tax law on state tax law with discriminatory extraterritorial effects. We found the reactions of foreign powers and the opinions of the Executive irrelevant in fathoming congressional intent because Congress had taken specific actions rejecting the positions both of foreign governments, *id.*, at 324-328, and the Executive, *id.*, at 328-329. Here, however, Congress has done nothing to render such evidence beside the point. In consequence, statements of foreign powers necessarily involved in the President's efforts to comply with the federal Act, indications of concrete disputes with those powers, and opinions of senior National Government officials are competent and direct evidence of the frustration of congressional objectives by the state Act.[23] Although we do not unquestioningly defer to the legal judgments expressed in Executive Branch statements when determining a federal Act's preemptive character, *id.*, at 328-329, we have never questioned their competence to show the practical difficulty of pursuing a congressional goal requiring multinational agreement. We have, after all, not only recognized the limits of our own capacity to "determin[e] precisely when foreign nations will be offended by particular acts," *Container Corp. of America v. Franchise Tax Bd.*, 463 U. S. 159, 194 (1983), but consistently acknowledged that the "nuances" of "the foreign policy of the United States ... are much more the province of the Executive Branch and Congress than of this Court," *id.*, at 196; *Barclays, supra*, at 327. In this case, repeated representations by the Executive Branch supported by formal diplomatic protests and concrete disputes are more than sufficient to demonstrate that the state Act stands in the way of Congress's diplomatic objectives.[24]

IV

The State's remaining argument is unavailing. It contends that the failure of Congress to preempt the state Act demonstrates implicit permission. The State points out that Congress has repeatedly declined to enact express preemption provisions aimed at state and local sanctions, and it calls our attention to the large number of such measures passed against South Africa in the 1980s, which various authorities cited have thought were not preempted.[25] The State stresses that Congress was aware of the state Act in 1996, but did not preempt it explicitly when it adopted its own Burma statute.[26] The State would have us conclude that Congress's continuing failure to enact express preemption implies approval, particularly in light of occasional instances of express preemption of state sanctions in the past.[27]

The argument is unconvincing on more than one level. A failure to provide for preemption expressly may reflect nothing more than the settled character of implied preemption doctrine that courts will dependably apply, and in any event, the existence of conflict cognizable under the Supremacy Clause does not depend on express congressional recognition that federal and state law may conflict, *Hines*, 312 U. S., at 67. The State's inference of congressional intent is unwarranted here, therefore, simply because the silence of Congress is ambiguous. Since we never ruled on whether state and local sanctions against South Africa in the 1980s were preempted or otherwise invalid, arguable parallels between the two sets of federal and state Acts do not tell us much about the validity of the latter.

V

Because the state Act's provisions conflict with Congress's specific delegation to the President of flexible discretion, with limitation of sanctions to a limited scope of actions and actors, and with direction to develop a comprehensive, multilateral strategy under the federal Act, it is preempted, and its application is unconstitutional, under the Supremacy Clause.

The judgment of the Court of Appeals for the First Circuit is affirmed.

It is so ordered.

1. What does this decision tell us about the way trade deals are made and implemented and about how trade agreements can be changed?

2. Should states be able to shape their own trade policies? Why or why not?

CHAPTER 4

WHAT ADVOCACY ORGANIZATIONS SAY

Free trade and globalization intersect with a number of issues, including environmental safety, workers' rights, and preserving indigenous cultures. Trade is also one of the driving forces of economic growth and cultural change, impacting the lives of millions around the world. As a result, both topics stir up strong debates and opinions. There are even disagreements among advocates for free trade about what makes a deal viable and strong; the North American Free Trade Agreement (NAFTA) and the Trans-Pacific Partnership (TPP) are two free trade agreements that have generated a great deal of debate from both those in favor of free trade and those against. Whether advocating for or against free trade, people on both sides are making strong arguments about these complex issues and presenting interesting solutions to the concerns they raise. Ultimately they all highlight important concerns that need to be considered when formulating trade policy, discussing free trade as a model, and thinking about the way what we buy impacts the rest of the world.

EXCERPT FROM "A VISION OF GLOBAL FREE TRADE? THE NEW REGIONALISM AND THE 'BUILDING BLOCS' DEBATE," BY MICHAEL G. PLUMMER, *ASIA PATHWAYS: A BLOG OF THE ASIAN DEVELOPMENT BANK INSTITUTE*, DECEMBER 10, 2013

While the WTO Ministerial meeting in Bali in December may deliver on individual initiatives related to such themes as agriculture, trade facilitation and development, a major breakthrough on the "single undertaking" is far from sight. At the same time, mega-regional agreements are fast emerging as a key feature of the global architecture. This "new regionalism" could pose risks, but successful mega-accords will create a strong incentive for a global accord; hence, the "new regionalism" will arguably be a powerful "building bloc" that will ultimately support multilateralism.

MEGA-FREE TRADE AGREEMENTS ON THE HORIZON

The Trans-Pacific Partnership (TPP) and the Regional Comprehensive Economic Partnership (RCEP) are two mega-regional agreements notable for their sheer size, overlap, and comprehensiveness. Moreover, the 2010 APEC "Yokohama Vision" aims to bring together members of these groups into a Free Trade Area of the Asia-Pacific (FTAAP) with negotiations to begin in 2020. [...] If negotiations go according to plan, these mega-free trade agreements (FTAs) could be in place within ten years and completely in effect within twenty years.

The "noodle bowl" of Asia-Pacific bilateral FTAs is giving way to the economic logic of consolidated regional FTAs that not only reduce the negative effects of bilateral FTAs but are more conducive to production networks that have been driving trade and investment in the region. This "new regionalism" will cut costs associated with bilateral FTAs and has many advantages over noodle-bowl bilateralism. It offers great economic benefits and a vision of future of global free trade.

Besides the Asia and Pacific region, regional approaches are being taken all over the world. For example, the European Union is expanding eastward—Croatia joined in July—and has launched FTA negotiations with Japan and the US. It has FTAs under negotiation with Africa under the Cotonou Agreement. The African Union has endorsed negotiations for a pan-Africa FTA—the Continental Free Trade Area—to be completed by 2017. Latin America has several sub-regional agreements in place and has expressed interest in a region-wide agreement, including possibly with North America under the Free-Trade Area of the Americas initiative (on hold since 2005).

THE FUTURE OF GLOBAL FREE TRADE

The Asia and Pacific region is the key to a global accord. A successful conclusion to the TPP negotiations will likely increase the incentives of Northeast Asian economies to work together with Southeast Asian economies to conclude the RCEP by 2015. If both are concluded, the Asia and Pacific region will be well on its way to an FTAAP by 2020. This process could potentially incentivize other regions and economies to move forward in a similar fashion, among themselves and with countries in the Asia and Pacific region. Recognizing this potential, negotiators will keep in mind the need to promote rules and standards that can optimally be multilateralized. In sum, if managed correctly, Asia and Pacific regionalism arguably offers the most promising path toward global free trade.

1. Why is Asia and the Pacific an important trade zone?

2. How can free trade be used best in this region? What are some of the problems posed by globalization?

"FREE TRADE: HISTORY AND PERCEPTION," BY STEPHEN DAVIES, FROM THE FOUNDATION FOR ECONOMIC EDUCATION, MARCH 1, 2006

In the natural sciences, such as physics, there is a large number of statements that can be made about the world that command general assent from scientists and those with a scientific education. This is not true to anything like the same degree in the human and social sciences, such as economics and history. The reason for this is the nature of their subject (human beings and their interactions) and the consequential inability to perform controlled and repeatable experiments.

Nevertheless, there are some statements about human beings and the social world that can be made with almost as much certainty as those concerning the natural world. One of these is the principle of comparative advantage and the consequent argument that a policy of free trade, even if followed unilaterally, will act to maximize both human cooperation and material well-being. This is one of the few things on which almost all economists agree, however much they differ in their politics and philosophy or position on other economic questions. Moreover, it is a proposition that has overwhelming empirical support: the brute facts of history resoundingly confirm that free trade increases output and leads to closer cooperation and economic integration among people, often those who are widely separated physically.

Despite this, however, the wider public does not share the economists' confidence in the principle. The case for free trade, which economists regard as overwhelming and as certain as is possible in the social sciences, has to be constantly remade in each generation. The contrary case, for protection and local self-sufficiency, has a continuing appeal and frequently carries the day in politics, often with disastrous results. There are a number of reasons for this, not least that the argument in favor of free trade is counterintuitive for many and that the costs of the policy are concentrated and visible while the benefits are frequently widespread and diffuse. However, there are two other related reasons that go a long way to explaining public thinking about this question: 1) the perception of trade as taking place between groups or political entities rather than individuals, and 2) the misunderstanding of history that follows from this. These date back to the first formulation of the idea of comparative advantage and still obscure what is actually at issue in the continuing argument.

Although earlier authors, such as Adam Smith, had pointed out the benefits of unrestricted trade and commercial intercourse, it was the British economist David Ricardo who first articulated the classical argument for free trade on the basis of comparative advantage in 1812. The idea that a part of the world should specialize in producing those products in which it had an absolute advantage was well established by then. What Ricardo did was to show with a simple mathematical argument that it paid for parts of the world to specialize in particular products even if they did not have an absolute advantage; that is, even if the same goods could be produced more cheaply elsewhere. The critical factor was their comparative cost in terms of alternative products forgone.

Ricardo's argument was quickly accepted and remains so among economists to this day. However, the way he presented his argument contained a basic flaw, which is the origin of the misunderstanding referred to earlier. He presented trade as taking place between countries rather than individuals. Quite simply, this is false. Countries do not trade with each other. It is individuals and corporate entities, such as firms, that do this. From the economic point of view, trade between persons in Maine and California is no different from trade between persons in California and Japan.

However, most people do not see economic life this way, and that is not how it is reported in much of the media.

Even more important is the way this distorts our understanding of economic history and the lessons to be learned from it. Two common arguments are made by critics of free trade. The first is that Ricardo's model assumes that capital will not move from one country to another. (Ricardo did indeed make this assumption, which is a consequence of his seeing the world of trade in terms of nations rather than individuals.) The second is that empirical history refutes the theory of free trade. The critics argue that the history of a number of nations, in particular the United States, shows that it is protection rather than free trade that brings about economic development and a rising standard of living while for most countries being integrated into a world of free trade means being condemned to low-value production and low incomes.

At first sight the evidence for the second argument appears strong. The United States moved sharply in the direction of a protectionist tariff policy after the Civil War and continued to follow this policy right up to the aftermath of World War II. During the same period (excluding the Great Depression and war years), the American economy grew rapidly and the United States became the world's greatest industrial power. How is this compatible with the argument that free trade is the best policy? The answer lies in realizing that trade is a matter of individual exchange rather than exchange between nations. Once you go beyond a society of completely self-sufficient households (if indeed such a thing ever existed) there will always be free trade. The question is not free trade yes or no, but rather how big is the area within which free trade takes place? The degree to which all participants will benefit from trade is a function of the extent of that area in terms of its geographical size and variety and the size and density of its population.

SUCCESS DEMYSTIFIED

This makes the success of the nineteenth-century United States easily understandable. The size of its territory and population made it the second largest free trade area on the planet, after the British Empire. Moreover, Britain's continuing free-trade policy reduced the negative effects of U.S. protectionism on the world economy. Looking at things in this way makes the current debates over globalization easier to understand in as much as we can see more clearly what the real issues are. We can also see that the first objection to Ricardo's model is invalid. As with trade, there is no meaningful economic distinction between a capital flow from, say, Somerset to Yorkshire and one from Yorkshire to Lisbon. The real question again is what the size and boundaries of the area within which capital flows should be. So what are the real issues at stake in the historical and contemporary arguments about trade? The basic one is: how far the economic and political units should coincide. The logic of economics is that if you want to maximize wealth and economic efficiency, then the unit of trade should be as large as possible, preferably the entire planet. Classical liberals argue that this will also bring social and political benefits, above all greater peace and interconnections between different parts of the world.

The most reasonable counter-argument is that this will lead to change that is too rapid, with consequent social instability and the destruction of settled ways of life, which will derail many people's expectations. Essentially, there is a tradeoff between greater wealth, comfort, and individual opportunity on the one hand and social stability and cohesion on the other. The choice is obscured, however, by a mistaken view of trade and the misleading perception of the world to which it leads.

1. How has the perception of free trade changed over time?

2. What role did free trade play in shaping the economic success of the United States in the twentieth century?

"FREE TRADE IS THE KEY TO ECONOMIC GROWTH," BY BARUTI LIBRE KAFELE, FROM THE FOUNDATION FOR ECONOMIC EDUCATION, OCTOBER 9, 2016

Typically when we watch the news, we are given a conspiracy theory of free trade economically strangling the American economy and destroying the economic plight of ethnic enclaves which are suffering financially like the African-American and Latino communities. This has even been a theme of the current presidential election. We are encouraged to believe that free trade is causing the loss of jobs in America and that it is leading to wide scale unemployment and impoverishment in the American economy. Many people complain about free trade without having an understanding of what free trade actually is. According to investopedia.com, free trade is:

> "The economic policy of not discriminating against imports from and exports to foreign jurisdictions. Buyers and sellers from separate economies may

voluntarily trade without the domestic government applying tariffs, quotas, subsidies or prohibitions on their goods and services. Free trade is the opposite of trade protectionism or economic isolationism."

Essentially, free trade gives global citizens the economic freedom to maximize or advance their economic interests as consumers, distributors and producers without government intervention. Hence, the globalization of commerce creates entrepreneurship, economic growth and innovation within a global society, while all protectionism, tariffs and isolation do is cause economic stagnation, unemployment and price inflation in domestic and global economies.

JOBS CREATED EXCEED JOBS LOST

One may argue that free trade has caused the loss of 5.6 million jobs in the manufacturing sector in the decade of 2000-2010. Ironically however, manufacturing output in the United States has increased by 40% in the past 20 years as the United States economy adjusted to the rate of inflation and produced twice as many products as they have done in any year since 1984! In an interesting paradox, while manufacturing jobs specifically within the textile industry have declined due to competitive prices in China, Bangladesh and other countries with cheaper markets, there has been an inverse result in productivity in United States' factories.

In 2015, the United States' output of durable goods reached an all-time high. These goods include refined petroleum products, plastics, electronics, aerospace goods, airplanes, chemicals, paper, pharmaceutical products, automobiles, etc. As technological advancement and overseas opportunities increasingly complement the laws of supply and demand, there are opportunities for employers to employ cheap labor overseas.

Ironically, the value of the United States' factories are approximately $2 trillion a year while the gross output of manufacturing industries consists of 36% of the country's gross domestic product. Hence, the manufacturing industries of the United States are worth more than the GDP of Italy, Brazil, and Canada separately. Hence, the opportunities for employment and entrepreneurship are definitely available within this country's borders in certain industries and also internationally.

At the same time, international workers can generate savings to start their own enterprises to compete with other factories that make manufactured goods cheaper, more durable and/or more efficient to produce. Additionally, international free trade gives U.S. consumers and entrepreneurs opportunities to contain consumption and productivity costs due to the competition of international factories—which creates opportunities for wealth accumulation and potential job growth in America.

The federal labor laws which include the minimum wage, minimum work hours, child labor laws and other regulations cause employers to look elsewhere in order for their products to get produced. The reason being is that these regulatory laws that have been enacted and ratified increase the costs of employment for employees whose productivity may not match their compensation and this causes the increase of losses for the businesses and creates the incentive to seek employment alternatives for the purpose of economic survival. Additionally,

businesses resort to technology to replace human beings
for the purpose of capital maintenance and commercial
efficiency. For example, at a local Capital One bank in
the city where I live in New Jersey, the branch decided
to terminate the bank tellers and replace them with ATM
machines, probably for the aforementioned reasons of
containing costs.

Hence, although technological advancement and
competitive products at competitive prices lead to the
loss of specific jobs, these technological advancements
also lead to the creation of new job opportunities.

WHAT HAPPENS WHEN THE GOVERNMENT IMPEDES FREE TRADE?

It is certainly not in the interest of a country for its government to implement protectionist or preferential policies to
penalize certain countries from trading with one another,
because this only leads to economic problems.

Donald Trump and Hillary Clinton are both vehemently
critical of job losses in the United States to China and other
countries. Trump, for example, calls for economic penalties
for companies like General Motors that outsource manufacturing jobs to Mexico. However, history has proven that
protectionism, tariffs and economic isolationism have caused
nothing but domestic economic problems and international
trade wars. A case in point is the Smoot-Hawley Tariff during
the Great Depression which was implemented during President Herbert Hoover's Administration in 1930 and which
implemented a 50% increase in import duties to protect the
American agricultural industry. This caused other countries
to take retaliatory measures that accelerated a 66% decline

in world trade between 1929 and 1934. Furthermore, this precipitated a major increase in U.S. unemployment—from 1.8 million to 12.6 million people.

FREE TRADE IS THE KEY TO GROWTH

International businesses, whether they are small and medium sized companies or large corporations like Sony, Toyota, Toshiba, Canon, Samsung, should not suffer just because governmental bureaucrats want to impose preferential policies to benefit certain companies in certain industries; nor should the American consumer who has demands and preferences for international products. All this does is impede overall economic progress mainly at the expense of the middle and lower classes, whether they are employed in a major corporation, involved in international business or are small entrepreneurs. Free trade enables a consumer to voluntarily purchase high quality products which are durable, affordable or sustainable from a producer in another country. Free trade is in the best interest of "the 99 percent."

Free trade is an answer to and ticket out of economic or cultural poverty and stagnation especially for traditionally economically disadvantaged groups in this country like African Americans, Native Americans, and Latinos. One should not get manipulated by politicians or presidential candidates like Donald Trump and Hillary Clinton who say otherwise. It is arrogant and paternalistic for governments to intervene in the contractual and economical affairs of competent parties who are engaging in commerce. If you have a problem with jobs being outsourced internationally, then you need to create or capitalize on the economic opportunities that abound in this age of globalization and technological advancement. It is by way of global trade, competition, opportunity maximization and consumer satisfaction that economic growth will happen in America through the creation of new jobs that can adapt to the technological changes.

In 1790, 90% of the American workforce was in the agricultural sector and today the sector accounts for only 3%. Therefore, it is modernization which leads to job losses in certain industries. As a result, it is up to you to adapt to economic and social changes in order to get a job in a thriving sector which demands your services and skills. If by chance you lack the skills, then you should consider training and education within that area of specialization. In light of the changes in the interactions between the consumer and producer, then it is up to you to create the job which suits the volatility and elasticities of the new economic dynamics.

In the final analysis, when prices are high and products in the United States are not comparable to those sourced internationally, then free trade is undeniably the best alternative.

1. According to the author, how does free trade promote economic growth?

2. What does the author blame for job loss?

CHAPTER 5

WHAT THE MEDIA SAY

The media play a key role in shaping the debate on free trade, largely by sharing how trade deals impact individuals through reported stories from around the world. In newspapers and on websites, the costs and benefits of free trade and globalization are discussed and debated by journalists, experts, and everyday citizens. Analysis provided by media outlets breaks down the complex issues and jargon involving free trade so that the public can understand what these deals mean. The media also provides an important outlet for those on the frontlines of trade deals—manufacturers, retailers, growers, and others engaged in the economy who are far removed from the halls of government. These people give us an understanding of how trade policy, including free trade, impacts people around the world. This wide range of perspectives and opinions makes the media an ever-changing reflection of how our world sees and is shaped by trade.

"FREE TRADE, GOOD OR BAD?" BY ROBERT A. LEVINE, *THE MODERATE VOICE*, MAY 3, 2016

With Trump and Sanders arguing against trade pacts, is free trade good or bad for the U.S. The United States in 2015 reached a deal with eleven other Pacific nations for a trade zone called the Trans-Pacific Partnership (TPP) to lower trade barriers and establish rules and regulations for the involved countries. Approximately 40 percent of the global economy would be included in the partnership. However, first it has to be approved by Congress as well as legislative bodies in the other participating countries. While this would be helpful in counteracting the commercial power of China, there is a lot of opposition in the United States, with unions fearing job losses and environmental groups concerned as well. There is also Republican resistance over providing President Obama with any sort of victory by voting for the TPP. Multinational corporations for the most part are in favor of the pact.

While free trade between nations would appear to provide significant benefits as shown by the E.U, there are problems that have to be worked out to truly reap these benefits. Though protectionist policies may temporarily save jobs in high cost countries, eventually products that are manufactured less expensively will command the marketplace. And though cheap labor may attract global corporations to certain countries, sophisticated workers may be required for particular jobs, increasingly so as work is performed by robots and computers. There is also the cost of transporting goods made in another country thousands of miles distant to the nation where the product will be used. Disregarding environmental protections to lower production costs will also come back to haunt nations that allow this. Health has been impaired in countries such as China that has to clean up the pollution in its air, soil, and water. Nations look after their own interests and global free trade will only become a reality when enough nations believe it suits them.

The bottom line is that there are winners and losers in free trade and trade agreements like NAFTA and the TPP. And years or even decades may be necessary to determine whether the benefits exceeded the damages for the nations that sign the agreements. Even economists have had difficulty deciding whether free trade helps developed countries or hurts them, though in the past, most thought that in the long run it was beneficial. As trade generally augments global economic output, economists believed that workers whose jobs vanished because of imports would rapidly find work in other fields that were expanding. Now, they are not so sure. Currently, there is much debate among economists over whether trade deals have been worthwhile for America. Previously, when trade was mainly between rich countries, labor costs were not that different from nation to nation. But trade agreements with nations whose labor is exceeding cheap compared to developed nations have been a different ballgame.

Many economists believe that the TPP will result in job losses and increased income inequality in all the participating nations, but even more so in the United States. There is little question that China, Japan, and Korea used America's desire for free trade for their own advantage over the years, protecting their own nascent industries and using currency manipulation to sell goods to the U.S. and other developed nations. And trade imbalances between China and the United States have continued, with exports from the U.S. much smaller than imports from China, giving the latter nation a persistent surplus. If exports to China had increased proportionately, with Chinese consumers buying imported products instead of saving their money, many more jobs might have been generated in America. That would have diminished unemployment and underemployment, along with some of the global trade imbalance. Trade agreements may have saved some American corporations' intellectual property and copyrights, and respect for some patents by foreign governments, but they did nothing for American workers.

Though the goods that came to America from China and other countries may have been cheaper than those made by American industries, and American consumers benefitted from this, many factories and businesses were ruined by the influx of these inexpensive products, and millions of workers lost decent-paying jobs. And even though some American products were sold to nations abroad through these trade agreements, there was pressure to keep prices down to compete with cheap labor in other countries. This resulted in diminished wages for those American workers who kept their jobs. Multi-national corporations and their executives did well with these trade agreements, but the average worker, particularly those who were uneducated, were badly hurt. Government programs for further education and retraining for different fields have not been adequate to salve the wounds of those who lost jobs and the reasonable wages they were earning. And it should be remembered that it was American companies like Walmart that were importing the products from China and other low-wage countries to heighten their own profits, disregarding the effect it would have on American workers.

Donald Trump on the right and Bernie Sanders on the left have used rhetoric that resonates with the disaffected middle and lower classes, white men with high school educations or less, who are now unemployed or unable to find well-paying jobs that would propel them back into the middle class. But the candidates' promises to bring factory jobs back from Mexico or China ring false. The jobs will not return even if the factories do. Trump's idea of 45 percent tariffs on Chinese products and breaking NAFTA will accomplish nothing for American workers but will raise prices for consumers. With factories increasingly automated globally, those that once employed five hundred workers, may now be able to function well with five or ten workers to see that the robots and computers are running smoothly.

It is no different than mega-farming where mechanization has cut the number of men and women needed to pick vegetables. Fifty years ago, 45,000 workers were required to pick and sort 2.2 million tons of tomatoes for ketchup in California. In 2000, only 5000 workers were necessary to harvest 12 million tons with the machines that had been developed. As farm output has skyrocketed, employment in that sector has fallen in the U.S. during the 20th century from 41 percent to 2 percent. Manufacturing employment can be expected to follow a similar course, no matter what the politicians say. At present it encompasses 8.5 percent of non-farm jobs, down from 24 percent in 1950, and may have further to go.

Though changes in trade policy may not make a significant difference in manufacturing employment, developed nations including the United States should try and maintain as much manufacturing domestically as possible, even with the smaller number of workers that will be utilized. However, de-industrialization in advanced countries means transitioning to a service economy, with well-paying jobs that require at least some level of education or training. Funds for retraining will have to come from government, industry, or both. In the United States, neither the Republicans nor the Democrats have paid enough attention to the travails of unemployed disaffected workers, stoking populist anger that has yet to be assuaged. Perhaps now, their angry voices will begin to be heard.

1. According to the author, what are some of the benefits of free trade? What are some of the disadvantages?

2. Who is the most affected by trade deals? How can they be protected?

"FAIR TRADE COFFEE A BIG BUSINESS, BUT INDIGENOUS GROWERS NOT GETTING RICH," BY MARLENA SAUCEDA, FROM THE CRONKITE BORDERLANDS PROJECT, SEPTEMBER 25, 2014

A cup of organic fair trade coffee begins in places like the 2.5 acres of highlands forest where Mariano Saramanco Gutierrez has been growing coffee almost all his life.

Saramanco Gutierrez's coffee plot, inherited from his parents, is a short walk down the road from his small home. It is spread across two hillsides separated by a small creek. The shrub-like coffee trees vary in width and height and are interspersed throughout the tropical cloud forest, set in between larger trees that drip with dew even as the day nears noon.

Saramanco Gutierrez shows off one plant, full of large, dark-green leaves and covered in bunches of green or red coffee cherries. Then he moves down the hill to another plant. Just a few spotted leaves cling to it; cherries hang on the thin, bare branches in groups of two or three. The plant is infected with "roya," rust fungus. Saramanco Gutierrez says that 90 percent of his plants have the disease.

In a good year, the 47-year-old indigenous farmer and his wife who helps him maintain and harvest the crop can earn around $4,000 for their organic fair trade coffee, the main source of income for the family of six. The rust means it might not be a good year.

Indigenous families like that of Saramanco Gutierrez are the backbone of Mexico's organic coffee industry. Coffee is grown in 88 of the 122 municipalities in Chiapas, and 45 of those are nearly 100 percent indigenous, Marco Antonio Botello Utrilla, a director in Chiapas' Institute of Coffee, said.

"One million people live off of coffee in Chiapas," Botello Utrilla said. That's slightly more than 30 percent of the population.

Of the 256,000 registered producers, which include cooperatives, civil societies, rural growers and plantations, two-thirds are made up of Mayan descendants like the Tzotzil, Tzeltal, Chuj and Zoque communities. While coffee is not native to Mexico, having been introduced by the Spanish in 1785, indigenous farmers have grown coffee on their own as a cash crop since the early 1900s.

The unstable nature of worldwide coffee prices has motivated these farmers to find a niche that would protect them from large drops in coffee prices: the organic and fair trade markets.

More organic coffee is grown in Chiapas, a Southern Mexico state slightly smaller than South Carolina, perhaps than anywhere else in the world. Sixty-four percent of the land devoted to organic-certified production in Mexico is in Chiapas, and Mexico is the world's leading producer of organic coffee, according to the U.S. Department of Agriculture's 2013 Global Agricultural Information Network report on Mexico.

The state began its revolution in coffee production in the late 1980s as organic and fair trade products gained popularity with consumers in Europe, the U.S. and Asia. As global coffee consumption rose, niche markets for specialty, high-quality coffees appeared, opening the door for a new, higher-paying market for small-scale indigenous farmers.

"As small producers, it's been a fight to win over the fair trade market over the last 20 to 25 years," Abraham Lopez Ramirez said. An indigenous producer himself, Lopez Ramirez is the president of the Museo de Café, a network of nine different cooperatives in the San Cristóbal de las Casas area.

"With our quality of coffee, we started to look for a market. It was principally in Europe where we began to take over niche markets. There they began to think, to encourage the idea that organic producers should be paid well, that they should get a fair price," Lopez Ramirez said.

This idea has allowed groups of indigenous farmers to create cooperatives and unions, systems through which hundreds of families pool their harvests together to export in large volumes. These groups worked together to obtain fair trade and organic certificates and now process and export their coffee, which ends up in posh cafes all over the world.

Saramanco Gutierrez belongs to the Maya Vinic cooperative, which was formed in the wake of the massacre of 45 members of a Roman Catholic support group known as Las Abejas—the Bees—in the impoverished indigenous community of Acteal in December 1997. Although they kept separate from the revolutionary Zapatistas who had rebelled against the government, Las Abejas professed support for some of the Zapatistas' goals. The 45 people, including women and children, were gunned down during a prayer meeting by members of a pro-government paramilitary group. No one was ever convicted.

The massacre drew worldwide condemnation and left the community struggling to find a way to move forward.

The answer, said Reynaldo Arias Ruiz, one of the four directors of Maya Vinic, already was on their land.

"We had to work, the community had to work to survive with their families," Arias Ruiz said. "The idea was that they had their plot, they had their coffee, their corn, their beans. The first objective was coffee because we here in Chiapas, we only find money when we sell coffee."

In 1998 they arranged their first export. Farmers came from around the area to join and sell coffee. Importers came from around the world to help by buying coffee. Individuals arrived from Japan and Switzerland and offered to establish connections between Maya Vinic and purchasers around the world.

"Solidarity groups came directly to Acteal to support us. Individuals came, in solidarity, to help. They supported our production by buying our product. That's how we found coffee purchasers in different countries," Antonio Ruiz Perez, another of the directors, said.

The tragedy of the massacre ultimately led to the globalization of Maya Vinic's business, giving its farmers a steady source of income year after year.

The marketing process begins when Saramanco Gutierrez and other members of the cooperative walk to the warehouse with their ripened coffee cherries in small sacks throughout the harvesting season. The cooperative pays them a base price that is agreed upon at the beginning of the coffee season. If the price rises by the time the coffee is processed, packaged and exported, farmers receive more money.

This year the price paid to farmers has averaged out to about 45 pesos per kilogram, a little less than $4 for a kilogram—2.2 pounds—of coffee cherries. It is a higher price than usual because worldwide coffee prices rose dramatically this year, nearly doubling from mid-February to mid-March. Usually farmers are paid from 29 to 35 pesos per kilo, Maya Vinic director Mariano Perez Vasquez said.

"It isn't enough to support their families for the whole year," Perez Vasquez said. "It's annual work to clean it, care for it and, when the harvest comes, to cut it with their families. We don't have schedules, we leave at 6 in the morning and, if we have to, we don't return until 6 in the evening. Here we are poor, and we have to work from sun to sun. That's what the indigenous have always done."

Smaller farmers, some with less than an acre of land who produce as few as 50 kilos per year, often rely on the cooperative for support.

"Supporting the smaller amongst the larger, that's what being a cooperative is about," Perez Vasquez said.

The rust fungus that is just now hitting the highlands where Maya Vinic's members live will greatly reduce the amount of coffee that producers are able to harvest and sell. It also means that the infected plants will need to be removed and replaced with new, young plants of a strain that is able to resist the rust.

Arias Ruiz said the cooperative has taken seeds from the resistant plant to sprout seedlings, tiny plants that they nurture at the cooperative headquarters before distributing them to farmers in need. It will take a year to replace the old plants with the new and two to three years for the new plants to mature before they produce good cherries. It will likely be five years before farmers who were hit hard, like Saramanco Gutierrez, are able to reach their full production volumes again.

The cooperative and its members face many challenges that go beyond infestations like the rust fungus. They compete directly with local intermediaries, people known derisively as "coyotes," who buy coffee directly from growers and sell it to multinationals.

These coyotes aren't registered with the government the way Maya Vinic is, so they don't pay taxes and they aren't certified organic or fair trade, meaning they don't pay for the certifications either, Perez Vasquez says. Buildings covered in painted words offering to buy coffee dot the roads from San Cristóbal de las Casas to the highlands. The coyotes can sometimes pay a higher price than the cooperatives in the area. When they can, farmers sell to them instead, even when they're members of a cooperative like Maya Vinic.

"We don't want them to sell to the intermediaries, but they go with the price," Perez Vasquez said.

Because of the way fair trade works, it only makes a substantial difference when coffee prices are low or drop unexpectedly. Purchasers pay a base price of at least $1.40 per pound. There is a 30-cent organic premium and a 20-cent social premium that is added onto that, Lopez Ramirez said. Usually cooperatives can get an extra 2 to 5 cents per pound for quality. This means that the lowest price organic-certified fair trade producers receive is $1.90 per pound. Occasionally, coyotes can pay 5 to 10 cents more than that.

Although individual farmers don't receive the extra help of the organic and social premiums when they sell to intermediaries, they would still rather get the higher price, since they immediately see the return.

"The strength of fair trade ends when [the price] rises above 140 cents per pound," Perez Vasquez said.

Whatever the price, Maya Vinic workers gather coffee cherries at their warehouse in Acteal, where they soak, dry and process them in a mill that removes the green pergamino beans from their shells and sorts them by weight and color. They gather them in 60-kilogram sacks and stack the sacks until it's time to export them. The sacks are driven nearly 240 miles to a seaport in Veracruz, where they are packed into shipping containers and put on a ship to New York City.

Monika Firl is the producer relations manager at Montreal-based Cooperative Coffees, the only importer of Maya Vinic's coffee in the U.S. Firl was living in San Cristóbal de las Casas and working with coffee cooperatives at the time of the Acteal massacre. She had established a relationship with Maya Vinic prior to the massacre and remained in contact with them after moving to Montreal in 2001, where she began working for Cooperative Coffees.

By then, Maya Vinic was preparing its first export. But a buyer in South America who promised to buy all of their stores for a great price backed out of the deal, leaving Maya Vinic wary of arranging another sale to a foreign buyer. Firl, however, already had established a high level of credibility with the cooperative and was able to facilitate Maya Vinic's first export to the U.S.

"Our motivation was everything they've been through and how important a steady source of revenue was for them," Firl said. "We were wanting to be in support of their struggle and recovery because they're good people and they produce quality coffee … to be able to offer them $1.46 per pound when the market price was 80 cents was amazing for them."

The business partnership between Maya Vinic and Cooperative Coffees began in 2001, before Maya Vinic had a fair train certificate. Then coffee market prices were very low and fair trade prices could make the most difference. From 2004 to late 2010 global market coffee prices remained below $1.50 per pound before skyrocketing to a market high of $3 per pound in early 2011.

During periods of low prices Cooperative Coffees' minimum price to producers is $2 per pound. When prices are extremely high, as they were in 2011, or above $2 per pound, as they are now, the importers base their purchasing price off of the worldwide market and then add on the social, organic and quality premiums. But they can't afford to double their price when the market price is at $3, Firl said.

Preventing producers from selling to coyotes for slightly higher prices is a shared responsibility between Maya Vinic and Cooperative Coffees, Firl said. The temptation for producers to get about 5 pesos more per pound is high, so the cooperative must maintain good relationships with their producers, even when market prices are high.

"They have to keep the co-op strong because the market will go down again," Firl said.

While Firl said that it's difficult for her to judge whether the lives of the members of Maya Vinic have improved because of her personal relationship with them, she acknowledged that Maya Vinic producers are still very poor. There are larger political and social challenges in Chiapas that the cooperative must deal with, she said.

"They live in remote areas, some of them still have dirt floors, some of them still don't have potable water," Firl said. "It's not like this has solved their problems … but it's something to hold on to, a little part of their lives that they can control."

Since 2001, Maya Vinic has exported an average of five containers of coffee to Cooperative Coffees every year. This has added up to a total of 1.045 million pounds.

"We could purchase three or four more containers from them [per year] if they could meet the demand," Firl said.

And the demand for their coffee is growing.

Some of the roasters who buy Maya Vinic's coffee from Cooperative Coffees have visited Chiapas. They not only admire the quality of the coffee but appreciate the story behind it.

"It's just a very dramatic story, and it's true and it illustrates what's possible. They have overcome a lot," Firl said.

Firl says that their minimum price to roasters is $2.85 per pound of green pergamino coffee. Roasters across the U.S. give Cooperative Coffees purchasing schedules of how much coffee they want and when they want it and the importers meet those demands. Roasting companies receive the coffee, roast it and sell it either as single-origin or blend it with other kinds of beans.

Mark Glenn, an owner of Conscious Coffees, a roasting company in Boulder, Colorado, said he has been buying Maya Vinic coffee from Cooperative Coffees for more than 10 years.

The coffee, Glenn said, is "overwhelmingly popular" with the cafes, grocery stores and consumers.

Because of coffee's seasonal nature, they only stock Maya Vinic's coffee, which they market as their Organic Mexico roast, for eight or nine months out of the year. When they don't have it in stock, Glenn says, he gets frequent calls from buyers asking when they'll have it again.

While the flavor and body of the coffee is very good and consumers like it, Glenn said he likes to think that its popularity is due to a loyalty that consumers feel to Mexican producers, neighbors of the U.S.

Glenn said that many of their loyal buyers are aware that by purchasing fair trade coffee from indigenous farmers, they are supporting remote, impoverished communities. He said, however, he doesn't think they understand how poor the Maya Vinic producers continue to be, despite the fair trade label.

"The vast majority of our consumers do not have the ability to empathize with the living standards of the producers," Glenn said.

Conscious Coffees and other roasters have made efforts to spread awareness about the struggles of the cooperatives. They've started a "roya fund" to provide Maya Vinic and other Latin American cooperatives with financial support while their production volumes, and incomes, take a hit from the fungus.

If production levels at Maya Vinic drop, however, roasters like Cooperative Coffees will turn to other sources to meet the demand for organic coffee from Latin America. Organic coffee from Honduras, Peru, Bolivia and other Mexican and Central American regions can replace the Maya Vinic roasts and consumers will still be satisfied, Firl said.

Brian Buckley, co-owner of Innisfree Poetry Bookstore and Cafe in Boulder, agreed that he has other options to serve his customers.

As an all-poetry bookstore and cafe across the street from the University of Colorado campus, Buckley said the cafe he and his wife opened in 2010 has a steady customer base. They've remained open, he said, because they carry locally roasted Conscious Coffees. While they bring in revenue from book sales, 60 to 70 percent of their revenue comes from coffee.

The organic Mexico roast is one that customers are "glad and excited" to see when they walk in, Buckley said, since the cafe rotates coffees every morning.

He said they will monitor the impact of the rust fungus to see what the cafe can do to help. Whether that means he'll charge more for the organic Mexico roast or just make extra efforts to educate his customers Buckley is not yet sure.

In the meantime, the Maya Vinic fair trade coffee is a hit. It may be loyalty to Mexico or seen as a way to keep families together or the sweet, chocolaty flavor that drives customers to buy Maya Vinic's coffee, Buckley said. But when long-term relationships with farmers are discussed, Chiapas and Maya Vinic always come up.

Many of Buckley's regular customers, like Joe Bryan, care to know where their coffee is coming from. For Bryan, a 40-year-old geography professor at the University of Colorado, walking into Innisfree and ordering a cup of organic, fair trade coffee from Chiapas is a political statement.

Bryan said that he likes to be able to buy coffee where he can follow the chain back to the grower. Everywhere he's lived in the U.S., he said, he's had places to go to get high quality, fair trade coffee.

"Fair trade tastes far better," Bryan said.

If organic coffee from Chiapas is available fewer months of the year, Bryan doesn't think it will have much of an effect on his daily life. He also doesn't think that means he's indifferent to the plight of the farmers in Chiapas.

Bryan said that as an educator and a person who has traveled to Chiapas and other impoverished coffee-producing areas, he has a different perspective on fair trade than most members of the niche market. While Conscious Coffees and Innisfree Cafe make efforts to educate customers on the still-dire living conditions of fair trade coffee producers, they can't do much to combat consumer complacency.

"They're vulnerable to the fact that someone comes in, buys coffee, sees a photo of a smiling coffee picker in country X and thinks they've done something good … but they haven't," Bryan said.

Bryan said that in recent years he's adopted a much more critical take on fair trade but still prefers it to coffee that is sold with no mention of the social aspects behind the production of the commodity.

Back in Chiapas, Saramanco Gutierrez said he does think selling coffee with Maya Vinic is better than it was selling to the coyotes.

As he walked back to his simple stone house where his wife and children work on different tasks in the muddy yard, he said he's not sure what he'll do until his coffee plot is healthy again.

"I grow corn and beans to eat," he said. "But I'm going to have to buy more corn this year. It's also not growing well."

1. How has fair trade impacted indigenous farmers?

2. Fair trade is often seen as an alternative to free trade. Based on this, compare and contrast the two approaches.

"THE WEALTH OF NATIONS AND THE FAILURE OF GLOBALIZATION," BY JAZZ SHAW, FROM *THE MODERATE VOICE*, FEBRUARY 9, 2010

While it remains depressingly futile to bang the drum of warning against the dangers posed to the American economy by the new "global economy" there is a piece up at HuffPo this week by Thom Harmann which everyone should read. Globalization Is Killing The Globe: Return to Local Economies

The reason I find the subject depressing (which, not coincidentally, is also the reason I get beaten up by my hard core conservative cronies on this) is that there are aspects of it which are glaringly obvious, but have become so politically poisonous among doctrinaire conservatives and party gadfly types that we're just not supposed to talk about them. Hartmann's piece is far from perfect, but it does provide a much needed refresher course on some economic fundamentals taken straight from one of the nation's earliest authorities on economics.

> "A stick on the ground has no commercial value, but if you add labor to it by carving it into an axe handle—a thing of commercial value—you have "created wealth." Similarly, metals in the ground have no commercial value, but when you add labor to them by extracting, refining, and forming them into products, you "create wealth." Even turning seeds and dirt and cows into hamburgers is a form of manufacturing and creates wealth.

> "This is the "Wealth of Nations" that titled Adam Smith's famous 1776 book.

"On the other hand, when a trader at Goldman Sachs makes a "profit" trading stocks, bonds, or currencies, no wealth whatsoever is created. In fact, to the extent that that trader takes millions in commissions, pay, and bonuses, he's actually depleting the wealth of the nation (particularly to the extent that he moves his money offshore to save or invest, as many do).

This definition is at the heart of the argument over what actually constitutes the fabric and soul of a potentially thriving American economy, or a fading, failing one. It addresses the question of how much of a burden is placed on the economic engine by people who, as my friend Ron Beasley has often put it, create profits by "*rubbing two pieces of paper together.*"

Unfortunately, Hartmann goes a bridge too far when working out his definitions of "income" vs. "wealth" as such analysts are frequently wont to do, but his argument is worth including here as a starting point.

""Wealth" is different from "income." Wealth is value, which endures at least for some time. Income is simply compensation for work. If you wash my car for $10 and I mow your lawn for $10, we have a GDP of $20 and it looks like we both have income and economic activity. But no wealth has been created, just income.

"On the other hand, if I build your car, I'm creating something of value. And if you turn my lawn into a small farm that produces food we can all eat, you're creating something of value. Not only do we have an "economy" with a "GDP," we also have created wealth.

Hartmann's unfortunate example takes a good starting point and shoves it off a cliff. In reality, all "work" performed as honest labor toward a productive end contributes to the overall "wealth." If you pay me to wash your car, I'm contributing to its maintenance, extending the useful life of the product and bolstering its potential resale price, thereby increasing the actual "value" of the car over its lifetime, albeit in a small way. Similarly, if you mow my lawn, you contribute to holding up the property value over time, increasing the value of the home. Going back to his example of sticks and ax handles, this is similar to saying that only the person running the wood lathe to carve the handles is creating "wealth." But what of the guy who mops the floors or the woman who changes the light bulbs in the factory and keeps power flowing to the lathe? They also contribute to the creation of wealth—in the form of ax handles—albeit indirectly.

The author would have done better to stick with examples of people who extract profit from the system by purchasing currency and waiting for its worth to fluctuate, sellers of junk bonds or, in one of the most common and extreme examples, cases where the government extracts tax money from the citizens and fritters it away without providing much real value to the taxpayer in return.

But that part is something of a distraction from the larger point, which Hartmann addresses here:

> "The main effect of the globalism fad of the past 30 years—lowering the protective barriers to trade that countries for centuries have used to make sure their own local economies are self-sufficient —has been to ship manufacturing (the creation of wealth) from developed nations to developing

nations. Transnational corporations love this, because in countries with lower labor costs and few environmental and safety regulations, it's more profitable to manufacture products. They then sell those products in the "mature" countries—the places that used to manufacture—and people burn through the wealth they'd accumulated in the earlier manufacturing days (home equity, principally, along with savings and lines of credit) to buy these foreign-manufactured goods.

"At first, it looks like a good deal to consumers in developed nations. Goods are cheaper! But over a decade or two or three, as the creation of real wealth is reduced and the residue of the old wealth is spent, the developed nations become progressively poorer and poorer. At the same time, the "developing" nations become wealthier— because those are the places that are producing real wealth.

Contrary to standard liberal dogma, the failing of our fiscally conservative, free market friends is not some sinister plot to prop up industries and the wealthy at the expense of the middle class. The problem is that our model is still based on a Happy Days mentality, treating corporate entities as if they still behaved the same way they did in earlier, happier times. We—and I include myself here —call for cuts in the corporate tax rate as the true path to economic recovery and job growth. And in theory this is the one true path. The federal government lacks the ability to actually "create" jobs in any long term, meaningful way which actually helps build and sustain the economy. The best they can do is create an environment where it is easier for private industry to grow and create those real jobs. Easing the tax burden on employers is a big part of that power.

Unfortunately, when constructing a strategy to put such proposals into place, the government must be aware that the corporate environment has changed radically over the last five decades and our policies need to reflect this if government action is to be effective. (My conservative friends should brace themselves now, because you're not going to like this next part at all.)

In the Happy Days, business models incorporating concepts such as international telecommuting were impossible. And nobody gave much thought to building factories or doing work in other countries which would help "foreigners" rather than our own citizens. It simply wasn't part of the American Dream. When the government took actions such as cuts in the corporate tax rate it hit the economy like a hot steroid injection. When new employees were hired, they were Americans. When a new factory went up, it was built in Boise, not Bangladesh. Further, competition was still vigorous. Companies worked to make a good profit, but they had to keep reinvesting in the business, resulting in further expansion, employment and general prosperity. The federal government could act boldly when it chose to do so and see direct results.

Globalization has not eliminated these effects entirely, but it has diluted them to dangerous levels. Competition has decreased and maximizing the bottom line on shareholder reports, dividends and executive bonuses is the order of the day. Workers are an expensive inconvenience to be reduced where possible and the cheap labor and raw materials which Hartmann references are too great of a temptation for virtually every business. Every extra dollar funneled into the economic engine by the government produces a drastically reduced return here at home in terms of jobs and prosperity.

So what is there to be done? Lest conservatives think I've taken leave of my senses, let me reassure you that direct government intervention and regulation is not the solution. That's simply not in keeping with the founding principles of the nation and leads us off on a different path to destruction. But the government can and should rethink their system of merit based rewards and incentives in their dealings with corporate America.

First, the government remains a huge consumer of privately produced goods and services. And they have every right to determine who they will or will not do business with. America First and Buy American should be the order of the day, with full preference given to companies who produce and hire here at home wherever possible. Also, the aforementioned tax relief will have far more of the desired impact if it is properly targeted. We should offer a more lenient tax rate to stimulate job growth, but offer it only to those companies who can demonstrate that they are repatriating offshore jobs and using domestically produced goods. For those companies who choose to continue the new age globalization practices, let them. The free market will still prevail. But offer them no cut in tax rates nor any other benefits. If they want to make their money overseas, let them see if they can find their customer base there as well.

Before we even get started on the response to this, let me anticipate it for you. "Protectionist!" my conservative cronies will cry. The "Smoot Hawley!" accusations will fly freely as if the speaker's hair were on fire. Protectionism? You are correct. That's become something of a dirty word in conservative circles, in case you didn't know, but we have something here which is badly in need of protection. Smoot Hawley? Please… spare me the Happy Days bleating. The failed policies of that era were badly implemented, but they were also fighting a very different enemy. Back then we were trying to stop other countries from flooding us with cheap products, materials and labor. The enemy today is of our own making and is found within our own borders. We are fighting to **keep** jobs here and to promote the use of **our own resources**, not defeat some perceived bogeyman from across the sea.

Some of these same critics will also declare that such policies will simply drive up prices for consumers. And yes, they are correct. You would have to pay more than one dollar for your roll of tube socks at Wall-mart. Hartmann provides the correct answer to this complaint as well.

> ""*But won't that make Wal-Mart's stuff more expensive*?" whine the flat-earthers.

> "Yes, it will. But most Americans (and Greeks and Spaniards) would gladly pay 10 percent more for the goods in their stores **if their paychecks were 20 percent higher**. And manufacturing paychecks have always been higher, because manufacturing is where "true wealth" is generated (thus the basis for most union movements, which further guarantee healthy worker income and benefits).

"The transnational corporations benefiting from globalization are also, in most cases, the transnational corporations that own our media, so even the word globalization is rarely heard in reports on economic crises around the world.

"But globalization is the villain here, and one that needs to be taken in hand and brought under control quickly if we don't want to see virtually the nations of the world end up subservient to corporate control, a new form of an ancient economic system known as feudalism.

The author's conclusion is a bit too dramatic for my tastes and festooned with hyperbole, but the underlying premise rings true. Circling back to the first paragraph, though, I am forced to finish this screed on a mostly dismal note. The path is there for us to take, but we're highly unlikely to pursue it. And the obstacles are not found in just one party or the other in Washington. Both have been complicit in this downward slide and the well financed interests who hold the leashes of the collection of lap dogs in Congress will not hear of any such reform. If you don't believe that, ask yourselves why there is no tort reform in the current health care bill or why Washington isn't even trying to eliminate the anti-trust exemptions for the industry which prevent competition across state lines? It doesn't take a genius to divine the answer. The people who fuel the system with cash don't want it to happen, so it doesn't. And they don't want us to reform the interface between government and business to promote real job growth and economic strength at home through America First policies, either.

1. According to the author, how has our perception of the economy failed to keep up with reality? What are some of the changes that have taken place?

2. How does the author feel trade should change?

"WHAT 'FREE TRADE' HAS DONE TO CENTRAL AMERICA," BY MANUEL PEREZ-ROCHA AND JULIA PALEY, FROM *FOREIGN POLICY IN FOCUS*, NOVEMBER 21, 2014

With Republicans winning big in the midterm elections, the debate over so-called "free-trade" agreements could again take center stage in Washington.

President Barack Obama has been angling for "fast-track" authority that would enable him to push the proposed Trans-Pacific Partnership, or TPP—a massive free-trade agreement between the United States and a host of Pacific Rim countries—through Congress with limited debate and no opportunity for amendments.

From the outset, the politicians who support the agreement have overplayed its benefits and underplayed its costs. They seldom note, for example, that the pact would allow corporations to sue governments whose regulations threaten their profits in cases brought before secretive and unaccountable foreign tribunals.

So let's look closely at the real impact trade agreements have on people and the environment.

A prime example is the Dominican Republic-Central America Free Trade Agreement, or DR-CAFTA. Brokered by the George W. Bush administration and a handful of hemispheric allies, the pact has had a devastating effect on poverty, dislocation, and environmental contamination in the region.

And perhaps even worse, it's diminished the ability of Central American countries to protect their citizens from corporate abuse.

A PREMONITION

In 2004 and 2005, hundreds of thousands of protesters filled Central America's streets.

They warned of the unemployment, poverty, hunger, pollution, diminished national sovereignty, and other problems that could result if DR-CAFTA were approved. But despite popular pressure, the agreement was ratified in seven countries—including Guatemala, Nicaragua, El Salvador, Honduras, Costa Rica, the Dominican Republic, and the United States.

Ten years after the approval of DR-CAFTA, we are seeing many of the effects they cautioned about.

Overall economic indicators in the region have been poor, with some governments unable to provide basic services to the population. Farmers have been displaced when they can't compete with grain imported from the United States. Amid significant levels of unemployment, labor abuses continue. Workers in export assembly plants often suffer poor working conditions and low wages. And natural resource extraction has proceeded with few protections for the environment.

Contrary to the promises of U.S. officials—who claimed the agreement would improve Central American economies and thereby reduce undocumented immigration—large numbers of Central Americans have migrated to the United States, as dramatized most recently by the influx of children from Guatemala, El Salvador, and Honduras crossing the U.S.-Mexican border last summer. Although most are urgently fleeing violence in their countries, there are important economic roots to the migration—many of which are related to DR-CAFTA.

One of the most pernicious features of the agreement is a provision called the Investor-State Dispute Settlement mechanism. This allows private corporations to sue governments over alleged violations of a long list of so-called "investor protections."

The most controversial cases have involved public interest laws and regulations that corporations claim reduce the value of their investments. That means corporations can sue those countries for profits they say they would have made had those regulations not been put into effect.

Such lawsuits can be financially devastating to poor countries that already struggle to provide basic services to their people, much less engage in costly court battles with multinational firms. They can also prevent governments from making democratically accountable decisions in the first place, pushing them to prioritize the interests of transnational corporations over the needs of their citizens.

THE MINING INDUSTRY STRIKES GOLD

These perverse incentives have led to environmental deregulation and increased protections for companies, which have contributed to a boon in the toxic mining industry—with gold at the forefront. A stunning 14 percent of Central American territory is now authorized for mining. According to the Center of Research on Trade and Investment, a Salvadoran NGO, that number approaches 30 percent in Guatemala and Nicaragua— and rises to a whopping 35 percent in Honduras.

In contrast to their Central American neighbors, El Salvador and Costa Rica have imposed regulations to defend their environments from destructive mining practices. Community pressure to protect the scarce watersheds of El Salvador—which are deeply vulnerable to toxic mining runoff—has so far prevented companies from successfully extracting minerals like gold on a large scale, and the Salvadoran government has put a moratorium on mining. In Costa Rica, after a long campaign of awareness and national mobilization, the legislature voted unanimously in 2010 to prohibit open-pit mining and ban the use of cyanide and mercury in mining activities.

Yet both countries are being punished for heeding their citizens' demands. Several U.S. and Canadian companies have been using DR-CAFTA's investor-state provisions to sue these governments directly. Such disputes are arbitrated by secret tribunals like the International Center for the Settlement of Investment Disputes, which is hosted by the World Bank and is not accountable to any democratic body.

In 2009, the U.S.-based Commerce Group sued El Salvador for closing a highly polluting mine. The case was dismissed in 2011 for lack of jurisdiction, but El Salvador still had to pay several million dollars in fees for its defense. In a case still in process, the gold-mining conglomerate Pacific Rim has also sued El Salvador under DR-CAFTA for its anti-mining regulations. To get around the fact that the Canadian company wasn't from a signatory country to DR-CAFTA, it moved its subsidiary from the Cayman Islands to Reno, Nevada in a bid to use the agreement's provisions. Although that trick failed, the suit has moved forward under an outdated investment law of El Salvador.

Elsewhere, Infinito Gold has used DR-CAFTA to sue Costa Rica for nearly $100 million over disputes related to gold mining. And the U.S.-based Corona Materials has filed a notice of intent to sue the Dominican Republic, also claiming violations of DR-CAFTA. These costly legal cases can have devastating effects on the national economies of these small countries.

Of course, investor-state disputes under DR-CAFTA are not only related to mining.

For example, TECO Guatemala Holdings, a U.S. corporation, alleged in 2009 that Guatemala had wrongfully interfered with its indirect subsidiary's investment in an electricity distribution company. Specifically, TECO charged that the government had not protected its right to a "minimum standard of treatment"—an exceptionally vague standard that is open to wide interpretation by the international tribunals that rule on such cases—concerning the setting of rates by government regulators. In other words, TECO wanted to charge higher electricity rates to Guatemalan users than those the state deemed fair. Guatemala had to pay $21.1 million in compensatory damages and $7.5 million in legal fees, above and beyond what it spent on its own defense.

The U.S.-based Railroad Development Corporation also sued Guatemala, leading to the country paying out an additional $11.3 million, as well as covering both its own legal fees and the company's. Elsewhere, Spence International Investments and other companies sued Costa Rica for its decision to expropriate land for a public ecological park.

A CHILLING EFFECT

What's at stake here is not only the cost of lawsuits or the impact of environmental destruction, but also the ability of a country to make sovereign decisions and advance the public good.

Investment rules that allow companies to circumvent national judicial systems and challenge responsible public policies can create an effect that's been dubbed "regulatory chill." This means that countries that might otherwise have curtailed corporate activity won't—because they're afraid of being sued.

Guatemala is a prime case. It's had to pay companies tens of millions of dollars in investor-state lawsuits, especially in the utility and transportation industries. But it hasn't yet been sued by a mining company. That's because the Guatemalan government hasn't limited the companies' operations or tampered with their profit-making.

Take the Marlin Mine in western Guatemala, for example. In 2010, the Inter-American Commission on

Human Rights advised the Guatemalan government to close the mine on account of its social and environmental impacts on the surrounding region and its indigenous population. Nonetheless, after briefly agreeing to suspend operations, the Guatemalan government reopened the mine a short time later.

In internal documents obtained by activists, the Guatemalan government cited potential investment arbitration as a reason to avoid suspending the mine, writing that closing the project could provoke the mine's owners "to activate the World Bank's [investment court] or to invoke the clauses of the free trade agreement to have access to international arbitration and subsequent claim of damages to the state." As this example demonstrates, just knowing that a company could sue can prevent a country from standing up for human rights and environmental protection.

More recently in Guatemala, the communities around San Jose del Golfo— about 45,000 people — have engaged in two years of peaceful resistance to prevent the U.S.-based Kappes, Cassiday, and Associates from constructing a new mine. Protesters estimate that 95 percent of families in the region depend on agriculture, an industry that would be virtually destroyed if the water were to be further contaminated. But the company threatened to sue Guatemala if the mine was not opened. "They can't afford this lawsuit," a company representative said. "We had a big law group out of [Washington,] DC fire off a letter to the mines minister, copied to the president, explaining what we were doing."

On May 23, the people of San Jose del Golfo were violently evicted from their lands by military force, pitting the government in league with the company against its own people—potentially all to avoid a costly lawsuit.

A PRELUDE TO THE TPP

Warnings about the crises that "free trade" would bring to Central Americans were, unfortunately, correct. Central America is facing a humanitarian crisis that has incited millions to migrate as refugees from violence and poverty, thousands of them children. One push factor is the environmental degradation provoked by ruthless mining corporations that are displacing people from their rural livelihoods.

And it's not just DR-CAFTA. The many investor-state cases brought under the North American Free Trade Agreement (NAFTA), and in countries all over the world, have exposed the perniciousness of investor protection rules shoehorned into so-called "free-trade" pacts. Many governments are realizing that these agreements have tied their hands when it comes to protecting their own environments and citizens.

We must use these egregious investor-state cases to highlight extreme corporate power in the region. We must work to help Central American people regain their livelihoods lost to ruthless extractive projects like mining. And we must change trade and investment agreements to stop these excessive lawsuits that devastate communities, the environment, and democracy itself.

Like DR-CAFTA, the proposed Trans-Pacific Partnership includes investor-state provisions that are likely to hurt poor communities and undermine environmental protections. Instead of being "fast tracked" through Congress, future trade agreements like the TPP—and the Transatlantic Trade and Investment Partnership being negotiated between the European Union and the United States—must be subject to a full debate with public input.

And such agreements must not, at any cost, include investor-state mechanisms. Because trading away democracy to transnational corporations is not such a "free trade" after all.

1. What has free trade meant for Central American economies? What good has it brought and what bad has it brought?

2. Based on the Dominican Republic-Central America Free Trade Agreement (DR-CAFTA), what are the author's concerns about the Trans-Pacific Partnership (TPP)?

CHAPTER 6

WHAT ORDINARY PEOPLE SAY

While trade deals are negotiated by the most powerful in a country, every citizen feels the impact of them. The perspective of ordinary people is important because it helps understand how trade deals, globalization, and other economic matters influence life on a day-to-day basis—from how much people are bringing home from work to what they buy at the supermarket. Manufacturers and retailers are impacted by decisions on where they can sell their goods and at what cost; consumers see it in what they can buy and for how much, as well as where goods come from in the world. Their views are often based on their own lives and the lives of those around them, offering portraits of American life across the country and how trade deals intersect with their experiences. Their stories and opinions add depth and reality to the debate on free trade and globalization, and can show how and why public opinion is changing.

"GLOBALIZATION'S CHALLENGE TO CITIES" BY BRUCE NESMITH, FROM *STRONG TOWNS*, JUNE 30, 2016

Last week's referendum in Britain on whether to remain in the European Union has been interpreted, at least in part, as a referendum on the increasing integration of economies across the Earth, which has accelerated in the last three or four decades. The phenomenon of globalization has been credited and blamed for a number of developments during this time; in fact while these developments might be caused by globalization, others are symptoms of a small world, the ability of economic power to buy political power, or mere coincidence. Globalization has certainly been associated with individual economic insecurity as well as the failure of state political institutions, and that has created volatile politics all over the world (Langfitt 2016).

From a troglodyte's perspective, the world began to globalize 3000-4000 years ago as trading developed across groups and, as navigation developed, across geographic regions. But that's not what we're talking about here. Technology has increasingly enabled manufacturing, marketing and, to a certain extent, service provision to occur across space without noticeable impact on the product or the consumer. No more is it enough to be the best bank, car dealer or bookseller in your part of town; now you're competing with banks, or car dealers, or booksellers all over the world.

In Thomas Friedman's felicitous phrase, today's world is "flat." Without going all in on his argument, the flatness metaphor is useful for illustrating how geographic barriers to competition have been removed, which makes economic security more difficult to achieve whether one is an individual, a firm or a city. Friedman, while noting that people "have to run harder to stay in place," generally sees this as a positive development, and he's far from alone in this. Tougher competition brings more and better choices for consumers, and all those firms and workers running harder will keep improving human life. Friedman emphasizes skill development as the answer to individual and national insecurity, particularly advocating improvements to the U.S. education system.

The benefits are hard to deny: Besides offering greater choices for consumers, a flat world has allowed development of a middle class in emerging nations like China and India, and reduced the extent of poverty worldwide especially in Latin America (FAO 2015). Of course, for the winners in global competition the rewards are huge. Just ask Jeff Bezos, founder of Amazon.com, who is probably the richest bookseller the world has ever known, or the heirs of Sam Walton, who founded the most dominant retail chain in history.

However, a lot of people, at least in the West, are finding that global opportunity cuts both ways, and are stressed by what seems like a loss of control over their lives (Berube). This insecurity is exacerbated by advances in automation, which allow manufacturing to be done by a fraction of the work force of days gone by; a liberal (at least in practice) immigration regime which flattens even local labor markets; and doubts about our ability to replicate the economic growth of the 20th century. (For the last point including its impact on politics and society, see Thomas Piketty, *Capital in the Twenty-First Century* [Harvard, 2014], ch. 2.)

What the forces of globalization, automation, immigration and slow growth have in common is that they raise questions about the future of work. The pop culture image of the blue collar working stiff slogging his way through the working day (think Johnny Paycheck's classic song "Take This Job and Shove It" or Fred Flintstone shouting "Yabba dabba do!" when the whistle blows at quitting time) seems positively blessed in retrospect. However boring, arduous or dehumanizing their jobs, that era's "blue collar aristocrats" could generally count on jobs being there for anyone able to work. If cars were going to be made, steel produced or coal mined from the Earth, large numbers of American (mostly) men were going to be needed to do it.

Previous technological advances have, of course, brought insecurity. The Luddite protests more than 200 years ago may not have been reacting to technological advances, but plenty of their contemporaries feared for their jobs in the Industrial Revolution (Conniff 2011). Eventually the descendants of the Luddites found work in mines, on railways, and in trades, joined unions and were paid reasonably well, and of course many people until relatively recently worked on farms (cf.Lebergott 1966). And maybe the answer to the future of work is just around the corner. Millions of jobs have been created since the depths of the recession in 2010, with the official U.S. unemployment rate falling from over 10 to below 5 percent.

However, there's a difference between a job and a career; wages remain stubbornly stagnant and long-term unemployment persists at a high level (Kille 2014, Burtless 2016). From the perspective of 2016, the future of work remains mysterious. If the current presidential campaign is any indication, political elites have less of a clue about what to do than I do, which unfortunately is saying a lot. It's little wonder that an insecure public turns on easy targets. If only we could ditch the EU bureaucrats, environmental regulations, or large banks; if only we could raise the minimum wage, restrict immigration, or make college free; then everything could go back to the way it was. Except somehow we'd get to keep all the cool stuff.

American cities today find themselves in a variety of positions. Some continue to reel from the collapse of the industrial economy four decades ago, and are struggling to serve citizens with multiple needs, stem declines in population, and figure out some way back onto the horse that is the global economy. Others have found their places in the global economy, as centers of technology, medicine, media and the like. But even those cities have a substantial number of poor citizens the benefits aren't reaching. Cities of all types are having to come up with policy solutions when [a] they are elusive, [b] past errors have left city finances in shaky states, and [c] people everywhere—not just Britain—are skeptical of government elites who collect taxes yet seem unable to deliver satisfactory outcomes.

I am no libertarian. I firmly believe that the answers to the problems of the 21st century will be found through conversation, building connections and collective effort. "We're all stuck here for awhile," as Rodney King once said. They will require government in order to articulate and administer collective decisions. But I'm not surprised that a lot of people react to the 21st century by sticking it to whomever they can—elites, phantoms, and each other.

1. How is globalization shaping cities?

2. What is the source of frustration with globalization we are seeing across the world?

"THE HIGH COST OF FREE TRADE," BY WILLIAM A. COLLINS, *OTHERWORDS*, JANUARY 23, 2013

NOT EVEN LEGISLATORS GET TO SEE DRAFTS OF SECRET NEGOTIATIONS OVER THE NEW TRANS-PACIFIC PARTNERSHIP.

Tidy rip-offs
From free trade;
For which we
so dearly paid.

The Trans-Pacific Partnership free-trade agreement, being negotiated in secret even as we speak, has a lot to say about worker rights and environmental protections. This pact, which is shaping up between the United States and 10 other nations, comes out squarely against them.

Like most other global trade deals, the true purpose of this so-called "partnership" is to "free" corporations from government rules, particularly those aimed at protecting us all from devastating pollution, barbaric working conditions, consumer fraud, and other forms of corporate abuse.

No wonder these negotiations are secret.

These deals are part of why modern global trade continues to rely on sweatshop-produced goods. Where would our proud nation be today without the world's sweatshops churning out the cheap goods that flood our homes? If those goods had to be produced under humane work rules and safety regulations, we couldn't afford them all. We'd have to get by with less stuff. Wait, wouldn't that be better for the environment, job creation, and the ever-daunting challenge of keeping all our possessions organized?

Sure, we've relied on cheap foreign goods for ages. But in recent decades, with the World Trade Organization, NAFTA, and other similar pacts, the benefits of this arrangement for most of us are shrinking. Governments understandably resist getting trapped between politically generous but grasping corporations on the one hand, and a cheated, abused, under-employed public on the other. Thus, they've shrewdly formulated international trade organizations to protect themselves from having to take the heat.

Take mining. Our Congress and Environmental Protection Agency may pass strict anti-pollution rules for American mines, but if a foreign owner buys up the pit and ignores the laws, he or she can often get away with it.

Such pillagers aren't subject to prosecution in U.S. courts, but rather to arbitration before WTO tribunals. There, they can successfully claim that stern anti-pollution laws unfairly deprive them of a reasonable profit under international trade rules. As a result, our government can only publicly wring its hands, while simultaneously winking at the smirking polluters. This goes on every day.

This pernicious system even works for tuna fish. The WTO has, for example, ordered Washington to halt the designation of "dolphin safe" on our cans. One of its tribunals found that such a label is unfair to Mexican fishermen who lack the special nets and the desire to avoid drowning dolphins.

And if the powerful United States loses cases like this, you can imagine how it goes in El Salvador, Paraguay, Zimbabwe, and the Philippines. Greedy politicians in those places long ago sold out their constituents to approve these trade treaties, and now they simply accept the results as a *fait accompli*. And frankly, our own history hasn't been all that different.

The secrecy surrounding negotiations over the new Trans-Pacific Partnership means that not even members of Congress get to see the drafts of the undemocratic deal brewing between Australia, Brunei Darussalam, Chile, Malaysia, New Zealand, Peru, Singapore, Vietnam, Mexico, Canada, and our own government.

But as always, there are leaks. One instructive disclosure obtained by Public Citizen informs us that of the agreement's 26 chapters, only two deal with trade. The other 24 codify various corporate rights and protections.

So, tell me. Whose interests will this pact serve?

1. Who does the author blame for the pitfalls of free trade?

2. What solutions does the author present to the issues he raises?

EXCERPT FROM "NAFTA AND FREE TRADE DO NOT BELONG IN THE SAME SENTENCE," BY DEAN BAKER, FROM THE CENTER FOR ECONOMIC AND POLICY RESEARCH, APRIL 17, 2012

[Note: Adam Ozimek wrote to tell me that the headline, "4 politically controversial issues where all economists agree," was not his. Without this headline, the blogpost is not especially objectionable.]

Megan MaCardle turned over her blog to Adam Ozimek to spread some misinformation about NAFTA and trade policy. Ozimek headlines the piece, "4 politically controversial issues where all economists agree." While I'm pretty comfortable with three of the four, the claim that all economists agree that, "the benefits of free trade and NAFTA far outweigh the costs" is highly misleading.

First, NAFTA was not about free trade. First and foremost, it was about reducing barriers that made U.S. companies reluctant to invest in Mexico. This meant prohibiting Mexico from expropriating factories and outlawing any restrictions on the repatriation of profits to the United States.

The agreement did little to loosen the obstacles facing highly-educated professionals in Mexico, like doctors and lawyers, from working in the United States. If the agreement had freed up trade in this area, it could have led to gains to consumers in the tens of billions of dollars a year.

In other areas, like patents and copyrights, NAFTA increased protection by extending the length and scope of these government granted monopolies. Mexico was forced to develop a U.S. type patent system for prescription drugs which led to considerably higher drug prices.

It is easy to see why someone who might in general support free trade would oppose NAFTA. The winners are the businesses that are in a position to take advantage of access to cheap labor in Mexico. The losers are the manufacturing workers in the United States who will now have to accept lower wages or lose their job.

It is entirely possible that an economist could agree that NAFTA did lead to net gains to the country as a whole, even if most people end up as losers (e.g. every worker loses $100 in wages, but Mitt Romney's clique pocketed an additional $50 billion in profit). In this case, she might say the policy was bad in spite of the net gains. (Several of the economists questioned raised exactly this concern.)

The higher costs imposed by higher prices for drugs and other products in Mexico could mean that a full assessment of costs would show Mexico to be a net loser from NAFTA. While tariffs are rarely more than 20-30 percent of a product's price, patents can raise the price of a drug by several hundred or even several thousand percent. The cost to Mexico's consumers in the form of higher drug prices can easily outstrip the small gains that showed up elsewhere. Of course this will lead to higher profits to U.S. drug companies.

Given the predicted distribution of gains, it is entirely possible that a fully informed economist could believe that the losses from NAFTA to the poor and middle class easily swamp the gains to the rich and for that reason oppose the policy. This is not bad economics as the discussion seems to imply.

Or, to put in terms that even an economist could understand, suppose there was a trade deal that completely opened up doctors, lawyers, and economists to international competition, but maintained the protection for everyone else, and hugely increased the protection for autoworkers. It is entirely possible that many economists would oppose this deal. They certainly would not call it a "free trade" agreement.

There is one final point worth making about this exercise. The line "all economists agree" carries much less weight these days because almost the entire economics profession somehow failed to see the $8 trillion housing bubble, the collapse of which wrecked the economy. Tens of millions of people continue to suffer with the loss of their jobs, their homes, and/or their savings as a result of this incredible incompetence.

In the wake of this momentous failure it is understandable that the public would be reluctant to take the advice of economists on economic policy. (Best question to ask an economist: when did you stop being wrong about the economy?) This is unfortunate, since economists really have learned some things from their studies that may not be apparent to everyone.

However, economists will have to earn back the public's trust. As long as economists pay no price in their careers for even the most disastrous failures, this may prove difficult. After all, if there are no consequences to getting things wrong, why would the public believe that economists will get things right? That is a point on which all economists should agree.

1. Why does the author argue that the North-American Free Trade Agreement (NAFTA) is not, in fact, a free-trade deal?

CONCLUSION

Trade has always been a driving force in our world, pushing us forward by bringing countries closer together and making it easier to share goods and culture. In the past century, the rapid increase in ease of travel and communication has brought about immense change in how we interact and share with the rest of the globe, thanks in part to free trade. For the United States, free trade now accounts for almost 50 percent of all international exports, bringing into the economy around $700 billion per year.[1] Along with that trade has come globalization, further bringing together people and cultures from different countries.

But many politicians, citizens, and lawmakers have concerns about the potential pitfalls of free trade and globalization, and there is a lot of debate about how trade agreements can take into consideration the many people who will be impacted by the deal. As we've seen, balancing economic growth with widespread well-being isn't an easy task and there are no simple answers to how to ensure all parties are satisfied with complex international trade negotiations.

In these articles, we've seen how free trade developed as a guiding force in international business and how our perceptions of free trade have changed with time. We've seen how lawmakers debate trade deals and how the courts approach questions of business interests in international trade. We've also seen how fair and free trade differ, and their impact on small farmers. From NAFTA to DR-CAFTA, we've gotten both sides of the debate on how these deals, and those like them, can both help economies grow and pose new challenges to countries. While trade and interaction between countries is key to maintaining a strong global economy, the shape that trade takes will be determined by the answers we find to the questions we've explored here.

BIBLIOGRAPHY

Baker, Dean. "NAFTA and Free Trade Do Not Belong in the Same Sentence." *Center for Economic and Policy Research*, April 17, 2012. http://cepr.net/blogs/beat-the-press/nafta-and-free-trade-do-not-belong-in-the-same-sentence.

Boehner, John. "Free People and Free Markets: A Vision for the Future of the Americas." *Speaker.gov*, May 8, 2012. http://www.speaker.gov/video/video-free-people-free-markets-vision-future-americas.

Chaisse, Julien and Qian Wang. "Was 2016 the Year the World Turned its Back on Free Trade?" *The Conversation*, January 16, 2017. https://theconversation.com/was-2016-the-year-the-world-turned-its-back-on-free-trade-67240.

Chang, Ha-Joon. "Kicking Away the Ladder: The 'Real' History of Free Trade." *Foreign Policy in Focus*, December 30, 2013. http://fpif.org/kicking_away_the_ladder_the_real_history_of_free_trade.

Collins, William A. "The High Cost of Free Trade." *OtherWords*, January 23, 2013. https://otherwords.org/the-high-cost-of-free-trade.

Davies, Stephen. "Free Trade: History and Perception." *Foundation for Economic Education*, March 1, 2006. https://fee.org/articles/free-trade-history-and-perception.

Ebeling, Richard M. "When the Supreme Court Stopped Economic Fascism in America." *The Foundation for Economic Freedom*, October 1, 2005. https://fee.org/articles/when-the-supreme-court-stopped-economic-fascism-in-america.

Greenspan, Alan et al. "Joint Letter in Favor of Trade Promotion Authority." *US House of Representatives Committee on Ways and Means*, March 5, 2015. https://waysandmeans.house.gov/UploadedFiles/CEA_Letter.pdf.

Kafele, Baruti Libre. "Free Trade is the Key to Economic Growth." *Foundation for Economic Education*, October 9, 2016. https://fee.org/articles/free-trade-is-the-key-to-economic-growth.

Levine, Robert A. "Free Trade, Good or Bad?" *The Moderate Voice*, May 3, 2016. http://themoderatevoice.com/free-trade-good-or-bad.

McCollum, Betty. "Congressional Record: H.R. 3087 Colombia Free Trade Agreement, H.R. 3079 Panama Free Trade Agreement, H.R. 3080 South Korea Free Trade Agreement, H.R. 2832 TAA and GSP Extension." *US House of Representatives*, October 12, 2011. https://mccollum.house.gov/press-release/congresswoman-mccollum-opposes-unfair-trade-deals-supports-trade-adjustment-assistance.

Nesmith, Bruce. "Globalization's Challenge to Cities." *Strong Towns*, June 30, 2016. https://www.strongtowns.org /journal/2016/6/29/globalizations-challenge-to-cities.

Ovin, Rasto and Pedja Ašanin Gole."Globalization, Governance, Democratization and Fair Trade, International Trade - On the Brink of Change." *InTech*, February 1, 2017. http:// www.intechopen.com/books/international-trade-on-the -brink-of-change/globalization-governance -democratization-and-fair-trade.

Perez-Rocha, Manuel and Julia Paley. "What 'Free Trade' Has Done to Central America." *Foreign Policy in Focus*, November 21, 2014. http://fpif.org/free-trade-done -central-america.

Plummer, Michael G. "A Vision of Global Free Trade? The New Regionalism and the 'Building Blocs' Debate." *Asia Pathways: A Blog of the Asian Development Bank Institute*, December 10, 2013. https://www.asiapathways-adbi.org/2013/12/a-vision-of-global- free-trade-the-new-regionalism-and-the-building-blocs-debate.

Rama, Martin. "Globalization and Workers in Developing Countries." *World Bank Development Research Group*, January 2003. http://documents.worldbank.org/curated /en/846921467988877048/Globalization-and-workers-in -developing-countries

Sauceda, Marlena. "Fair Trade Coffee a Big Business, But Indige- nous Growers Not Getting Rich." *Cronkite Borderlands Project*, September 25, 2014. https://cronkite.asu.edu/buffett/chiapas /fair-trade-coffee-a-big-business-but-indigenous-growers -not-getting-rich.

Shaiken, Harley. "The Impact of International Free-Trade Agree- ments on Job Growth and Prosperity." *Journalist's Resource*, January 15, 2015. https://journalistsresource.org /studies/economics/business/international-free-trade -agreements-job-growth-prosperity-impacts.

Shaw, Jazz. "The Wealth of Nations and the Failure of Globalization." *The Moderate Voice*, February 9, 2010. http:// themoderatevoice.com/the-wealth-of-nations-and-the -failure-of-globalization.

Sklair, Leslie. "Competing Conceptions of Globalization." *Journal of World-Systems Research*, Vol. 5, Issue 2, Summer 1999. http://jwsr.pitt.edu/ojs/index.php/jwsr/article/view/140/152.

Staff. "Remarks by President Obama and President Pena Nieto of Mexico in Joint Press Conference." *The White House*,

July 22, 2016. https://obamawhitehouse.archives.gov/the-press
-office/2016/07/22/remarks-president-obama-and-president
-pena-nieto-mexico-joint-press.
"Stephen P. Crosby, Secretary of Administration and Finance of
Massachusetts, et al., v. National Foreign Trade Council."
United States Supreme Court, from the Cornell University Law
School Legal Information Institute, June 19, 2000. https://
www.law.cornell.edu/supct/html/99-474.ZO.html.
Whitman, Marina v. N. "Want to Help Free Trade's Losers? Make
'Adjustment Assistance' More Than Just Burial Insurance."
The Conversation, October 24, 2016. https://theconversation
.com/want-to-help-free-trades-losers-make-adjustment
-assistance-more-than-just-burial-insurance-67036.

CHAPTER NOTES

INTRODUCTION

1. International Trade Administration. "Free Trade Agreements." http://www.trade.gov/fta.
2. Destler, I. M. "America's Uneasy History with Free Trade." April 28, 2016, *Harvard Business Review*. https://hbr.org/2016/04/americas-uneasy-history-with-free-trade.

CHAPTER 1: WHAT ACADEMICS, EXPERTS, AND RESEARCHERS SAY

"GLOBALIZATION, GOVERNANCE, DEMOCRATIZATION AND FAIR TRADE" BY RASTO OVIN AND PEDJA AŠANIN GOLE

[1] Norman, L. (2016) 'Growing Percentage of People Arriving in EU Are Economic Migrants, Commission Says. Jan. 26, 2016', *The Wall Street Journal*. Available at: http:// www.wsj.com/articles/growing-percentage-of-people-arriving-in-eu-are-economic-migrants-commission-says-1453815921 [16.8.2016].
[2] *See*: FINE (2001) *Fair Trade Definition and Principles*. Brussels: Fair Trade Advocacy Office.
[3] WFTO (2014) *Defining Fair Trade*. Available at: http://www.wfto.com/about-us/historywfto [28.7.2016]
[4] Bevir, M. (ed.) (2010) *Encyclopedia of Political Theory*. Thousand Oaks, London, New Delhi, Singapore: SAGE Publications, p. 491.
[5] Fairtrade Foundation (2016) *What is Fairtrade?*. Available at: http://www.fairtrade.org. uk/en/what-is-fairtrade [9.8.2016].
[6] cf. Harrison, B., Harris, J. and Deardorff, M. (2014) *American Democracy Now*. 4th ed. New York: McGraw-Hill Education.
[7] Ritzer, G. (2011) *Globalization: The Essentials*. Malden, Oxford, West Sussex: Wiley Blackwell, A John Wiley & Sons, pp. 295–297
[8] Johnson, D. (2016) 'President Tells Congress TPP Is Coming Their Way. What Will Clinton Do?', *OurFuture.org*, 12 August. Available at: https://ourfuture.org/20160812/ president-notifies-congress-tpp-is-coming-their-way [17.8.2016].

[9] Rosamond, B. (2007) 'Economic Governance', in Bevir, M. (ed.)
Encyclopedia of Governance. Thousand Oaks, London, New
Delhi: SAGE Publications, pp. 350–353.

[10] Stiglitz, J.E. (2003) 'We Have to Make Globalization Work for
All: Reforms of the Trade and Financial Systems are Impera-
tive', *YaleGlobal Online*. Available at: http://yaleglobal. yale.edu
/content/we-have-make-globalization-work-all [17.8.2016].

[11] Stiglitz, J.E. (2002) *Globalization and Its Discontents*. New York:
W.W. Norton & Company.

[12] cf. Crowther, D. and Aras, G. (2010) 'Overview: Globalisation
and Corporate Governance', in Aras, G. and Crowther, D. (ed.)
A Handbook of Corporate Governance and Social Responsibility.
Farnham and Burlington: Gower Publishing Limited, pp. 1–4,
and Ritzer, 2011.

"COMPETING CONCEPTIONS OF GLOBALIZATION" BY LESLIE SKLAIR

FOOTNOTES

5. For example, research on the idea of commodity chains, networks of labour, production and marketing of goods, has
shifted attention away from national economies to global
forces, to some extent (see Gereffi in Sklair, ed. 1994,
chapter 11).

6. See Stuart Hall's chapter 6 in Hall et al. (1992). Also relevant
here are Appadurai's five dimensions of global cultural flows:
ethnoscapes, mediascapes, technoscapes, financescapes,

7. This is quoted in many different places. My source is, significantly, from the back page of the 25th Anniversary Issue of
Earthmatters, the magazine of Friends of the Earth, UK. The
quote is superimposed on a very cloudy map of a rather pol-
luted planet earth.

8. I take this argument further in the section on 'Globalization in
Everyday Life' in Sklair (forthcoming).

9. For example, Strauss and Falk argue 'For a Global People's
Assembly' in the *International Herald Tribune*, (14 November
1997), a publication that advertises itself as the newspaper for
global elites!

10. Today, more or less every specialism in the social sciences has

its 'globalization' perspective, for example, globalization of
law, social welfare, crime, labour and politics. Among the most
important substantive issues, widely discussed by globalization
researchers inside and outside the four approaches outlined
above, are global environmental change, gender and globalization, global cities and globalization and regionalization,
discussed in Sklair (forthcoming).

REFERENCES

(place of publication is London unless otherwise indicated)

Albrow, M. (1996) *The Global Age*, Cambridge: Polity Press.

Albrow, M. and King, E. eds. (1990) *Globalization, Knowledge and Society*, Sage.

Alger, C. (1988) 'Perceiving, analysing and coping with the local-global nexus', *International Social Science Journal* 117, August: 321-40.

Barker, Chris (1997) *Global Television*, Oxford: Blackwell.

Barnet, R. and Cavanagh, J. (1994) *Global Dreams*, New York: Simon and Schuster.

Chase-Dunn, C. *Global Formation*, Oxford: Blackwell, 1989.

Dicken, P. (1998) *Global Shift: Transforming the World Economy Paul Chapman, third edition.*

Dowmunt, T. ed. (1993) *Channels of Resistance: Global Television and Local Empowerment*, BPI/Channel Four.

Dunning, J. (1993) *Multinational Enterprises and the Global Economy*, Wokingham: Addison-Wesley.

Durning, A. (1992) How Much is Enough, *Earthscan*.

Ekins, P. (1992) *A new world order: grassroots movements for global change*, Routledge.

Featherstone, M. ed. (1990) *Global Culture: Nationalism, Globalization and Identity*, Sage.

Giddens, A. (1991) *The Consequences of Modernity*, Cambridge: Polity Press.

Hall, S., Held, D. and McGrew, T. eds. (1992) *Modernity and its Futures*, Cambridge: Polity Press.

Harvey, D. (1989) *The Condition of Postmodernity*, Oxford: Basil Blackwell.

Held, D. (1995) *Democracy and the Global Order*, Cambridge: Polity Press.

Hirst, P. and Thompson, G. (1996) *Globalizationin Question: The International Economy and the Possibilities of Governance*, Cambridge: Polity Press.

King, A.O. ed. (1991) *Culture, Globalization and the World-System*,
Macmillan.

Mander, Jerry and Goldsmith, Edward eds. (1996) *The Case against
the Global Economy*, San Francisco: Sierra Club.

McGrew, T. (1992) 'A Global Society?', in *Hall et al. eds*. cp. cit.

McMichael, P. (1996) *Development and Social Change: A Global Perspective*, Thousand Oaks: Pine Forge Press.

Mlinar, Z. ed. (1992) *Globalizationa and Territorial Identities*,
Aldershot: Avebury.

Nordenstreng, K. and Schiller, H. eds. *Beyond National Sovereignty:
International Communications in the 1990s*, Norwood: Ablex.

Reddift, M. and Benton, T. eds. (1994) *Social Theory and the Global
Environment*, Routledge.

Ritzer, G. (1995) *The McDonaldization of Society*, Thousand Oaks:
Pine Forge, second edition.

Robertson, R. (1992) *Globalization: Social Theory and
Global Culture*, Sage.

Robinson, William (1996) 'Globalisation: nine theses on our
epoch', *Race and Class* 38 (2): 13 31.

Ross, R. and Trachte, K. (1990) *Global Capitalism: The New
Leviathan*, Albany, N.Y.: State University of New York Press.

Scott, Alan ed. (1997) *The Limits of Globalization*, Routledge.

Shannon, T. (1989) *An Introduction to the World-System Perspective*,
Boulder: Westview.

Sklair, L (forthcoming) 'Globalization: New Approaches to Social
Change', in S. Taylor, ed. *Contemporary Sociology*, MacMillan.

Sklair, L (1998a) 'Globalization and the Corporations: The case
of the California Fortune Global 500' *International Journal of
Urban and Regional Research* (June).

Sklair, L (1998b) 'Social movements and global capitalism' in
E Jameson and M. Miyoshi, eds. *Cultures of Globalization*,
Durham, NC. Duke University Press.

Sklair, L (1995) *Sociology of the Global System*, Baltimore: Johns
Hopkins UP, second edition (first ed. 1991).

Sklair, L ed. (1994b) *Capitalism and Development*, Routledge.

Spybey, T. (1995) *Globalization and World Society*, Cambridge:
Polity Press.

Sussman, G. and Lent, J. eds. (1991) *Transnational Communications:
Wiring the Third World*, Sage.

United Nations Development Programme (1993) *Human
Development Report* 1993, Oxford: Oxford University Press.

Wallerstein, I. (1979) *The Capitalist World-Economy* Cambridge:

Cambridge University Press.
Wallerstein, I. (1991) 'The construction of peoplehood: racism, nationalism, ethnicity'. In E. Bali bar and I. Wallerstein, eds. *'Race', Nation, Class*, Verso.
Waters, M. (1995) *Globalization*, Routledge, 1995.
Yearley, S. (1996) *Sociology, Environmentalism, Globalization: Reinventing the Globe*, Sage.

"GLOBALIZATION AND WORKERS IN DEVELOPING COUNTRIES" BY MARTIN RAMA

For references, please consult the original article.

"STEPHEN P. CROSBY, SECRETARY OF ADMINISTRATION AND FINANCE OF MASSACHUSETTS, ET AL., V. NATIONAL FOREIGN TRADE COUNCIL" FROM THE UNITED STATES SUPREME COURT

For references, please consult the original court decision.

CONCLUSION

1. International Trade Administration. "Free Trade Agreements." http://www.trade.gov/fta.

GLOSSARY

competition—In business and trade, a rivalry that drives retailers and manufacturers to be innovative, profitable, and active.

developing countries—Agricultural states that have small but growing economies.

exports—Goods sold to other countries.

fair trade—Trade in which fair prices are paid to the local producers of goods.

free market—An economic system with few restrictions on competition among private businesses.

free trade—Trade between countries without tariffs or other restrictions.

global economy The international trade of goods and services between countries.

globalization—The spread of culture, business, ideas, and goods between countries.

imports—Goods brought into a country to sell.

International Trade Administration (ITA)—A federal agency under the US Department of Commerce that handles nonagricultural exports.

interventionist—Government involvement in regulating the economy through ownership of production or other measures that go beyond measures like enforcing contracts or setting up trade agreements.

laissez-faire—A government policy of allowing the free-market economy to self-regulate without federal interference.

neoliberal—An economic ideology that favors free-market capitalism over protectionism or other economic approaches.

North American Free Trade Agreement (NAFTA)—A trade treaty signed in 1994 that established free trade between Mexico, Canada, and the United States.

protectionism—The opposite of free trade; policies that make it more difficult and expensive to trade with foreign countries, including tariffs and quotas on goods being imported or exported.

Smoot-Hawley Tariff—Also known as the Tariff Act of 1930, this law raised import tariffs to around 50 percent.

tariffs—Fees on imports and exports.

trade imbalance—A trade imbalance occurs when a country's imports are more highly valued than its exports, resulting in a deficit.

FOR MORE INFORMATION

Boskin, Michael J. *Nafta at 20: The North American Free Trade Agreement's Achievements and Challenges.* Stanford, CA: Hoover Institution Press, 2014.

Brown, Keith R. *Buying into Fair Trade: Culture, Morality, and Consumption.* New York, NY: NYU Press, 2013.

Crayton, Lisa A., and Laura La Bella. *Globalization: What It Is and How It Works.* New York, NY: Enslow Publishing, 2016.

Garten, Jeffrey E. *From Silk to Silicon: The Story of Globalization Through Ten Extraordinary Lives.* New York, NY: HarperCollins, 2016.

Hanson, Ann Aubrey. *Free Trade* (Opposing Viewpoints). New York, NY: Greenhaven Press, 2013.

Herschbach, Elisabeth. *Global Inequalities and the Fair Trade Movement.* New York, NY: Mason Crest, 2016.

Irwin, Douglas A. *Free Trade Under Fire.* Princeton, NJ: Princeton University Press, 2015.

Lemert, Charles. *Globalization: An Introduction to the End of the Known World.* Abingdon-on-Thames, UK: Routledge, 2016.

Levete, Sarah. *The Race to Fix the Global Economy.* New York, NY: Rosen Publishing, 2015.

Perritano, John. *Trade, Economic Life, and Globalization.* New York, NY: Mason Crest, 2016.

WEBSITES

International Monetary Fund (IMF)
www.imf.org
The International Monetary Fund is an international organization
promoting greater economic cooperation between nations;
more information about its projects around the world, as well
as economic data, is available on its website.

International Trade Administration (ITA)
www.trade.gov
This government agency works to promote US exports. It's
website offers information about trade deals and laws between
the United States and other countries.

World Bank (WB)
www.worldbank.org
The website of this international organization provides information about trade agreements and policy around the world.

INDEX

ABOUT THE EDITOR

Bridey Heing is a writer and book critic based in Washington, DC. She holds degrees in political science and international affairs from DePaul University and Washington University in Saint Louis. Her areas of focus are comparative politics and Iranian politics. Her master's thesis explores the evolution of populist politics and democracy in Iran since 1900. She has written about Iranian affairs, women's rights, and art and politics for publications like the *Economist*, *Hyperallergic*, and the *Establishment*. She also writes about literature and film. She enjoys traveling, reading, and exploring Washington, DC's many museums.